Why Should We

Every Day is an In.

2nd Edition

Brooks Harper

Why Should We Hire You?
Every Day is an Interview
2nd Edition

ISBN: 978-0-9853146-1-3
Library of Congress Control Number: 2017907559

Published by Brooks Harper Enterprises LLC
Book Cover Design by KarrieRoss.com

For Information Contact:
Brooks Harper
brooksharperspeaks@gmail.com
www.brooksharper.com

Published by Brooks Harper Enterprises LLC
Lexington, SC

Printed in the USA

ACKNOWEDGEMENTS

I'd be remiss if I didn't carve out a page in this book to acknowledge and thank some of the key people in my life and career who believed and invested in me.

My Mom, who worked tirelessly to provide a roof over our heads, put food on the table and raise us right.

My Wife, who builds me up and holds the whole thing together.

My children, Katelin and Dean for inspiring me.

David Campbell III at the Boys and Girls Clubs of the Midlands, who taught me personal accountability and many life skills.

Upward Bound Program at the University of South Carolina for showing me college was possible.

Matthew Miner Jordan who told me to never sell myself short.

Guy Jordan, who showed me the way.

Dr. Kaye Shaw and Lisa Call at for opening so many doors.

My former employers and present clients who remind me that every day is an interview.

Making it Count.

You, for being a gracious listener and applying what you learn.

TABLE OF CONTENTS

Introduction

DON'T Skip the Intro!
It tells the WHY behind the WHAT!

Much has changed since the first release of *Why Should We Hire You?* Not only have we experienced shifts in the job market, technology, hiring practices, search and effective interview strategies, but I have also observed changes in my own personal growth and development as a career expert and interview coach. Though I am not interviewing as an extreme sport as I did for years, I am working with a variety of clients who are in search of their dream job over a wide range of career fields. My philosophy on career search and interviewing practices has evolved and been refined to meet the needs of both young and seasoned, student and professional in the most competitive job market in history. With the development of countries like China and India and advances in technology and communication, now more than ever it is essential to employ the full extent of our reach and be creative and tenacious as possible in pursuit of meaningful employment.

It has been reported that India has more honor students than America has students. Translation: they have more smart kids than America has kids. And many students and professionals still don't believe this truth really has an effect on THEM. NEWS FLASH: IT DOES!

I was recently on a plane flying from Atlanta to Charlotte sitting beside a recent graduate from a university in India. With his 7 year work visa in hand, he was on his way to launch his career with a company in Charlotte, NC that employs approximately 180,000 people around the world. I found it interesting and sobering that the company didn't choose to fill this particular position with a graduate from UNC, NC State, Wake Forrest or Duke University, but hired a candidate 8000 miles away.

The job market has unprecedented competition. It is fierce and it is global. Consider the National Basketball Association and pay attention to the international flavor of the league. Team rosters now have over 100 international players from more than 40 countries. There was a time when the NBA draft primarily consisted of players from American colleges, universities and high schools. Now, it includes up and coming players from around the world. This global search for the best and brightest talent is not exclusive to the NBA, but extends to all career fields: education, finance, banking, medical, etc. The good news is: You can compete with the best and the brightest if you are prepared!

"Why should we hire you?" In 100 % of the interviews that I have been on, this was the last question I was asked in some form or fashion. If you're being asked this question in an interview, the following assumptions could be made: 1) Your resume or application was good enough to get a response, 2) you potentially passed a number of interviews, both phone and face to face, and 3) the company you are interviewing with is now seriously considering making you their final choice. Your response to this final five-word question will be pivotal in determining whether you hear "Welcome to the team" or "We have decided to move in a different direction." If you hear the second of these two responses, then it is typically followed up with something like this: "We will keep your resume on file, and will contact you should opportunities become available requiring someone with your skill sets." Allow your humble coach to translate this statement for you, "You will never hear from us again." The reality is that you get one shot at telling them why they should hire you, and your response is critical to receiving an offer. Some call it a two-minute elevator speech, while others call it a closing statement. Label it what you will, but understand, if you don't nail this portion of the interview, then the interview is over.

This book is written with the following purposes:

- To share strategies on HOW to develop your network and get in front of the person or people who make the hiring decision.

- To train you how to spot and avoid the pitfalls many fall into during their job search.

- To show you how to hit the toughest interview questions out of the park.

- To challenge you to think about the value you bring to an organization and what makes you different from the thousands of candidates applying for the position.

- To empower and enable you to articulate why a company should hire you in a clear, concise and compelling way that yields the following result: "When can you start?"

- To appreciate that "Every Day Is an Interview" and an opportunity to turn your passion into a paycheck and learning into earning.

Those who are successful at interviewing understand it is a combination of art and science, and no two interviews are ever the same.   There are fundamental tenets of interviewing discussed in this book that you need to be aware of, as well as some out-of-the-box approaches companies are taking in this needle-in-a-haystack environment of hiring the best candidate. When unemployment is at record highs, one would assume it would be easy for employers to find good quality people; on the contrary, it is now more difficult than ever for them to find the right person for the job.   Through conversations with many human resource managers and placement companies, I have learned the market is flooded with so much talent it has become increasingly difficult for hiring managers to decide on the best candidate, making it vital for you to be able to answer, "Why should we hire you?"

How many job applicants does it take to change a light bulb?
2000, but only one got the job!!!

Whether you are a teacher, high school student, college graduate, or mid-career professional, this book will prepare you to answer the tough questions, ask the right ones, and enable you to intuitively hit the "curve balls" out of the park. You will hear selected stories from countless interviews I have been on which have resulted in offer letters from Fortune companies to non-profit organizations.

This book will not give you "magic" words to guarantee a job offer on every interview. I have coached job seekers in the past, who thought they could take one of my stories and insert it into their interview—only to fall flat on their faces. It is written with the intent of helping you figure out what you are meant to do and put together a plan to help you achieve it. We are all at different points in our lives and careers, with various levels of education and experience. Regardless of your current status, this book should serve as a guide to help you get to where you aspire to be professionally.

This book will encourage you to seriously consider the talents, skills and experience you have, and how your personal stories can be packaged to market yourself to potential employers. Using the techniques outlined in this book in conjunction with your personality and intuition will put you closer to hearing, "You're hired!"

Chapter 1
Facts Tell, Stories Sell

When I conduct career workshops, I typically ask my audience this question, "By a show of hands, how many of you consider yourself to be a sales person?" Very few hands ever go up. Depending on my audience, I then say, "For those of you who raised your hands, thank you for your honesty. As for the rest of you....you're mistaken, and I will prove it to you. How many of you, when you were younger, convinced your parents to buy you something?" Without exception every hand goes up. "How many of you have ever convinced your spouse to do something for you?" Without exception every hand goes up. "How many of you have ever convinced a teacher or professor to move back a deadline on a paper or an assignment?" At this point the response is predictable, to which I say, "Welcome to the Sales Department." Everyone is selling something! I was in the mall with my daughter, and she asked, "Daddy, do you want to go to Starbucks before or after lunch?" She didn't ask me if I wanted to go to Starbucks, she phrased the question to produce the result she wanted, regardless of how I answered. Either way, she gets Starbucks! She's in sales. When you interview with a company, you are simply selling yourself! The quicker this concept is grasped, the better off you are going to be and the closer to getting the job of your dreams!

Sometimes it seems people have a negative connotation with being forced to sell themselves. If you are uncomfortable with the concept of selling yourself, then I want you to set this book down for a moment, go the door and see how many employers are lined up outside waiting to hire you. If no one is there, then I encourage you to pick this book back up and keep reading. If there is a line outside your doorstep, you'll still need this book to help close the deal and negotiate your compensation package. Welcome back to reality! Never hesitate to tell companies why you are the best person for the position. The person interviewing after you certainly isn't going to come in and convince them why they should hire you. You have to sell yourself!

I was watching a newscast that spoke of a new phenomenon called a "quarter-life crisis." I am sure that you are familiar with the term mid-life crisis. This is when dad hits 50 and goes out and buys a new convertible or Harley. The term, "quarter-life crisis", is used to describe recent college graduates who have always been told, "Go to college, and you will get a great job," only to graduate and find themselves unemployed and back at home with their parents. In many cases they are unemployed because they bought-in to the notion that going to college guaranteed them a job. When their sense of entitlement has been hit head on with reality, a quarter-life crises occurs. After 4-5 years in college preparing for a career, real life education begins with "TANSTAAFL" (there ain't no such thing as a free lunch). If you want your dream job, education is not enough. For those of you in a quarter, mid, or third quarter life crisis, here are a few tips:

1) If you want something in life you have to go after it. Stop going to the door expecting employers lining up to hire you.

2) You are the best product that you have to offer. Learn to sell it.

...wood is good, but vinyl is final...

When I graduated from college, I walked across the stage with thousands of other graduates. The president of the university put a diploma in one hand, shook the other, and I was suddenly thrust into the "real world." Instead of networking and taking full advantage of the Career Center at school, I mistakenly decided to do it the hard way. (Take full advantage of the resources at your disposal. The Career Center is one of the best, but unfortunately one of the most underutilized.) I reviewed job listings and found a job that said, "$400/wk guaranteed." I picked up the phone and called, and within a few moments I had scheduled an interview for the next day. I showed up the following day along with thirty other eager people looking for $400 guaranteed. We were all hired. The fact that everyone who showed up that day was hired should have been an indicator that this might not be the best job opportunity. After the third day in my new position, I figured out that I was now a vinyl siding sales person. My job would be to go into homes throughout the state and convince owners to convert their wood siding to vinyl. The company's slogan was, "wood is good, but vinyl is final." I soon learned the "$400/wk guaranteed" wasn't exactly a paycheck. It was what the company called a "draw."

This is how it worked: The company would let us borrow $400 each week until we sold something, and then would take it back out of our commission once we made a sale. On that first Friday at the end of the day, I was looking forward to having that $400 in my hand, even if it was a loan. That's when they told me that the $400 draw wouldn't start until I had been employed for 30 days. After two weeks of beating the streets and going into homes that should have been condemned, I turned in my scratch resistant samples to look for employment more suitable for me.

A couple of days later, I received a call from a friend. Having learned of my plight, he let me know his company had an open position and wanted to know if I would be interested in applying. (The best opportunities are going to come your way through your personal and professional network. See Chapter 2 Interviewing Is a *Contact* Sport). He gave me the hiring manager's information and said he would put in a good word for me. It was my responsibility to contact the manager and set up the interview. I made the call and scheduled the interview for the following day.

You can imagine that after a failed attempt at selling vinyl siding, and with student loan payments becoming due, I was under pressure to produce some income. I put on my best shirt, tie, slacks, and shoes, got in my car and headed off to the interview. On the ride over, I was listening to sports radio while thinking about some of my accomplishments and things that might set me apart from everyone else. The broadcasters were discussing one of the most compelling stories in sports history. As I listened to the story, I got the idea that, if packaged correctly, I could use it as an illustration to help set myself apart from the other candidates.

When I showed up for the interview, the receptionist took me back to the manager's office. There were two managers in the office waiting for me. Though I needed this job, I wasn't nervous in the least. While in high school and college, my affiliation with the Boys and Girls Club provided me opportunities to speak to a wide range of audiences, large and small, in a variety of venues, to diverse groups of people. Those speaking experiences have proven to be invaluable in interviews, business, and a host of other areas of my life regarding communication.

I felt the interview went well. It was one of those days when I was on a roll. Every question they threw my way, I hit out of the park. Nothing could stop me now. At the end of the interview, I asked what they thought of my interview. By asking this question, I learned that I had interviewed well. They said I had many of the skill sets necessary to be successful with their company. They thought I would be a good fit for the position, but there was another candidate equally as strong. They were considering either hiring him or me and would call me in the next two days with their decision.

...facts tell, stories sell...

As they stood up to walk me to the door, the managers asked if I had anything else I would like to say. I politely asked them to sit back down, and proceeded with the following illustration which has proven to be legendary in its own right. As they sat back down, I said, "In 1984 the Portland Trail Blazers had the #2 pick in the NBA draft, do you know who they picked? Neither manager had a clue.

I said, "Sam Bowie. Fortunate for the Chicago Bulls who had the #3 pick that year. They chose Michael Jordan, and the rest is history! Championships, rings, trophies, all the things that go along with being a part of a championship team, Chicago enjoyed, because they hired the right person." At this point I wasn't sure if they knew where I was going with this illustration, but I definitely had their attention.

I continued, "But I want you to consider Portland for a moment. The Portland Trailblazers had the opportunity to acquire the greatest basketball player to ever play the game…"

I paused and looked at my hands and said, "You know? Portland let that opportunity to draft Michael Jordan slip right through their fingers."

I looked both of them in the eye and said, "Don't be Portland! Don't let me slip through your fingers!"

I got up and showed myself out. Two days later they called and offered me the job. I went to work for them for a number of years, quickly moving through the management ranks.

I often look back at that interview and laugh. When I walked out of their office that day, I put them in a position where they had no choice but to hire me. To let me "slip" through their fingers possibly meant competing against me at a later date.

History had shown what making the wrong choice cost the Trailblazers, as one of M.J.'s six championships came at Portland's expense.

Sometimes you have to take a bold approach to set yourself apart from other people. After years of interviewing others and being interviewed, I've learned that landing a great job is both art and science. This is chess, not checkers. You have to be strategic, intuitive and know when to take a chance.

Towards the end of every interview; I always ask these two questions:

1) **How did I do?** I ask this to uncover any concerns they may have about hiring me. This usually gives me an opportunity to make sure all of their concerns are addressed.

2) **Where do we go from here?** This question lets me know if there are other steps in the process and how many other decision makers there may be. It also can reveal how serious they are about hiring me. Remember, as long as you're in the interview you have an opportunity to convince them why you are the best candidate. Don't save your best stuff for the interview you give in the car on the ride home. Leave it all on the table, but don't over sell it either.

...In order to G-E-T you have to A-S-K...

In order to GET you have to ASK! I once sent my resume off to one of the largest pharmaceutical companies in the world, applying for a sales representative position. A human resources representative called me and asked me 10 screening questions. When she finished asking her questions, I asked her what the next step would be. She told me that they had received over 2000 resumes from the job posting. Out of these resumes, they chose 40 to call for the initial screening. Of the 40 candidates she was calling that day, only 10 would be chosen to move forward for a face-to-face interview with the hiring manager. She let me know I was fortunate to be one of the 40 selected to be screened and that I would be contacted if chosen to be one of 10 interviewed. As she was ending the call, I told her I wanted to be one of the 10 people interviewed. I explained that I needed an opportunity to convey to the hiring manager why I felt I was the best candidate for the position. She scheduled my interview right then on that initial call. I later found out that if a candidate didn't **ask** to be a part of that next interview, then they didn't **get** an interview. It's one of the techniques they used to weed out the 40 candidates called that day.

Recently I was coaching someone who was looking to change careers. She was fortunate to get a phone screen with a company she had applied to. She called me afterwards to let me know the screening interview went well. I asked her what the screener said the next step in the process would be. She was told they were just calling the initial candidates and would be getting back in touch with the three or four best for a face-to-face interview. I asked her if she made a push to be one of the candidates to move forward in the process. Her response to me was that the person calling her was only someone from human resources and would not be making the final hiring decision. I agreed with her, but countered that this person would be the deciding factor in who would move forward in the interview process. I reminded her that she should always ask to move forward, and I wished her the best. I checked back with her two weeks later to get an update on how things were going. Unfortunately, she still had not heard from them, and I assured her that she wouldn't.

In order to G-E-T you have to A-S-K! In order to get you have to ask! So many job applicants do very well in the interview and forget to do the most important and fundamental thing: ASK FOR THE JOB! ASK TO MOVE FORWARD! All they can do is tell you "no." You must be vigilant in asking to move forward and be ready to give strong reasons why advancing your application is in the company's best interest.

There are so many factors, variables, and moving parts in the interview process, but with the right combination of information, commitment, planning and action, you can land the job you have always wanted, or the job you need until you find the job you have always wanted. I base this thought on the following belief:

> **Everyone's life has purpose, and we all have talents, skills, and abilities necessary to fulfill this purpose. Knowing this, it is your responsibility to develop your talents, skills and abilities through experience and education. You also have to be ready to tell your**

story to whoever is sitting across from you at the interview table. The last question they are going to ask you is, "Why should we hire you?" and you have to be ready and able to communicate your value in a way that convinces them you are the one.

While conducting a career workshop, I asked a participant who seemed somewhat disengaged what he planned to do in the future. Confidently he said, "I really don't need this workshop, because I'm going to be an engineer."

I said, "Oh really? Let me ask you a question. When you show up to interview with your engineering degree after you graduate college, guess what the other 40 people who are interviewing that day will have?"

He said, "What?" I said, "They will have an engineering degree, too. And if you don't have your story straight and some of the things that I am talking about in this workshop to set you apart, then you are going to be OTD." He said, "What's OTD?"

I said, "Out the door! And on the way out the door you may hear this: Thank you for coming in today. We will compare you with the other candidates here today and be back in touch."

"Translation: You will never hear from us again." You get one shot at an interview, and you have to make the most of it. He sat up in his chair and re-engaged.

If you have equal candidates with similar education, experience and skill sets, the individuals who do the best job of articulating their strengths, and how those strengths will benefit the company, are going to be in a much better position to win the job. Making a simple, broad statement that you are a "people person" in an interview is not enough. What companies want to hear is how you can use your interpersonal abilities to leverage results for them.

So if facts tell and stories sell, then you need some stories to tell. Do not say to yourself that you don't have a story to tell, because everyone does. Unless your story is you've been a lazy bum the past several years and have spent the majority of your time watching television, streaming video, and gaming, then you have a story to tell.

...past behavior is a predictor of future performance...

I am a big proponent of stories, not only because they are easier to tell than answering interview questions, but stories are what employers are looking for during an interview. As a manager with more than 10 years of hiring experience, I am thoroughly trained in Targeted Selection and Meticulous Hiring practices. Both of these interview philosophies require applicants to provide specific examples of things they have done that show how well they have performed in previous situations. The theory is that the manner in which you have behaved in the past can predict how well you will perform for them in the future. Answering these types of questions as if you are telling a story eliminates much of the pressure and anxiety that interviews can produce. This approach allows you to be genuine, natural, and show them the real you. Many people dread the thought of answering grilling interview questions, but most would be perfectly comfortable in telling a story about themselves. That's all interviewing is: Telling your story in a manner that persuades someone to hire you.

In Chapter 4 we will discuss in greater detail the types of questions you may get in an interview, but typically these questions are "Tell me about a time" scenarios. The interviewers will ask you to tell them about a specific instance when you did or accomplished something. They will expect you to explain the specific situation or task you were in, the actions you took, and the results of your actions. An acronym for this is "STARs" (Situation/Task, Actions, Results). Scenario style questions will deal with topics related to the skill sets they are looking for in a candidate. For example, if the company is looking for a highly organized individual, you may be asked a question like this:

> "Tell me about a time when you were extremely busy, handling multiple tasks; and your life was very hectic. Regardless of how busy you got, you were able to step back from the situation, organize, and prioritize without letting anything go undone. Tell me the situation you were in, the actions you took and the results of your actions."

This is a lot different than, "How do you stay organized?" For many people, this is when the temperature in the room seems to increase by 15 degrees; they begin to sweat, and it feels like their mouths are stuffed with cotton balls. In this scenario, you will be required to recall a specific situation that occurred in your previous experience, explain the details of what took place, the specific actions you took to manage the situation, and the ending results of the actions you took. Interviewers will be watching closely for contradictions and whether or not you switch from what did happen to a hypothetical statement. If your answer is not consistent, or they have to keep asking you to tell them specifically what you did instead of what you would do, this can adversely affect the quality of your interview. For instance, a wrong way to respond to this scenario would be:

> Well, there was a semester in college when I was taking 18 credit hours, working a part-time job and doing community service work. If something extra came up then I would typically..........

STOP!!! The answer started out describing a specific situation that took place one semester in college. However, in the second sentence it went from specific to hypothetical and generic. At this point, professional interviewers would have to stop you and ask what you specifically did in the situation you are describing. Below is a better example of staying consistent with your story of how you stayed organized:

> Well, there was a semester in college when I was taking 18 credit hours, working a part-time job and doing community service work. Realizing I was spinning so many plates, I became concerned that I might miss a deadline on a term paper or get the schedules mixed up at work, so I installed a scheduling app on all of my devices. I began to schedule all of my classes,

assignment due dates, work hours and to-do lists on the app. The app has notifications to alert me that tasks are coming due. When I implemented this system, my life became so much easier to manage and I was able to keep my commitments without letting anything slip through the cracks. I continue to use this highly effective system today.

In this response, a clearly stated situation has been given, actions have been taken to mitigate the situation, and the outcome of the actions taken have been shown. Simply put, it's telling the story of how you stayed organized. Your interviewers now understand how you have organized in the past which indicates how you may stay organized in the future.

Stories are so much easier to tell than answering interview questions. When you reduce your answers to telling a story, it takes the pressure off of you and you stay a lot dryer and a lot less thirsty in the interview. It becomes less of an interview and more like professionals having a conversation and sharing best practices.

Now it is time for you to start thinking about your stories. Think about the things you have accomplished during the course of your life and career, both academically and professionally. Think about the most trying times in your life and what you did to overcome those adversities and win. Later in the book you will see questions which will require responses from you and your stories. Based on these questions you will need to look back into your past experiences and remember actual situations you were in that would satisfy and speak to that particular topic. You will want to be able to clearly and concisely discuss the specific situation, action taken and results of your action.

Think about events and times in your life when YOU:

- led others to accomplish a goal
- changed someone's mind or opinion
- worked as a team to get something accomplished
- had to re-prioritize
- felt you were treated unfairly
- received negative feedback
- faced conflict at work
- disagreed with a decision your company made
- were wrong
- took initiative at work or school

In each instance, remember to be clear and concise. Once you have the stories on paper, practice telling them out loud. When it comes to "touchy" subjects, make sure you "OWN" it. Don't make excuses, justify poor behavior, whine or point the finger at someone else. Take 100% responsibility and hold yourself accountable. When you admit mistakes without excuse and then discuss how you moved forward and overcame them, you set yourself apart because it's refreshing and rare for someone to do so.

Your stories will sell YOU to the company you're interviewing with. Have your stories straight and be ready to share them confidently and sincerely.

POTENTIAL CURVE BALL

An associate of mine was halfway through an interview once when the hiring manager said, "Let me see your wallet." This struck him as an unusual request. Nevertheless he pulled out his wallet. Fortunately for him, he had a small wallet that only held credit and debit cards. If he had pulled out a wallet barely closable, overflowing with receipts, he would have lost credibility no matter how good his "How I Stay Organized" story was.

Action Items and Reminders from Chapter 1

1) If you want your dream job, you have to go after it. Don't expect employers to be lined up to hire you.

2) You are the best product that you have to offer. Learn to sell yourself.

3) At the end of every interview and at every phase of the process always ask, "How did I do?" and "What is the next step?"

4) Always ask to be a part of the next step in the interview process, and be prepared to tell them why they should move you forward in the process.

5) Write your stories down to answer potential questions which may be asked to describe your skill sets, making sure they cover the situation, action and result.

6) Practice telling these stories to other people, or record yourself telling them, and play them back to yourself.

Chapter 2

Interviewing Is a *Contact* Sport

You can be a master at interviewing, but it's worthless unless you can get in front of the hiring manager to actually tell your story. Gaining the opportunity to present why you are the best fit for the position can be one of the toughest aspects of obtaining meaningful employment. When a resume or application is submitted online, the employer's software is loaded with filters that weed out candidates, producing a quality pool of applicants to move through additional screenings. This software could be programmed to check for education level, years of experience, certifications, languages spoken, salary expectations, etc. If your application or resume does not have one of the requirements the position calls for, the filters in the software block your application from moving forward. This is why many of the applications and resumes submitted online are never seen by the human eye. In addition to filters, many companies will have applicants complete a number of assessments to determine aptitude in a particular area as part of the initial application process. These assessments could include keyboarding competency, mathematical ability, reasoning skills, and personality traits. If a certain score is not achieved on these assessments, the application is filtered out.

In a globally competitive job market you must use every advantage at your disposal to get in front of the hiring manager. This may include using your personal and professional contacts to put you in the interview chair. Often friends or acquaintances within the company can use their influence to get your resume into the right hands for consideration. Getting as close to the decision maker as possible may help bypass a ton of red tape, making your resume less of a needle in a haystack. Never underestimate the power of your personal network and contacts to produce new opportunities. Whether you are a recent high school or college graduate, or seasoned professional looking to shift gears, your friends and associates can't help you unless they are aware of your situation.

Prior to resumes and applications being submitted online, it was standard practice to mail your resume with a cover letter, list of references, and salary history to the human resources department. I know of individuals who stapled dollar bills to their resumes in an effort to make them stand out above the others. Let's assume you were a hiring manager and had to look through a stack of 500 resumes and pull out the top ten. Chances are if you came across a resume with a dollar bill stapled to it, you would at least give it a second glance. But in this day of web applications it is much more difficult to get your information to stand out. That is why using your network to get an interview is so important.

Interviewing is a *contact* sport. You have to leverage every personal and professional contact at your disposal to put yourself in front of the hiring manager or decision maker. Unfortunately, many view the term "networking" in a negative light. Far too many people think it disingenuous to set out to meet people with the end goal of furthering your career. This is the wrong mindset to have. Not only can the people you meet help you achieve your career goals, but you may be able to help them as well. The networking door swings both ways. Those who are uncomfortable with networking typically find themselves underemployed, complaining about the people who networked their way to the corner office.

...Those not networking, often are not working...

Get LinkedIn!

One of the best ways to connect with professionals and build your network is through the professional networking site, LinkedIn. Not only does it allow you to create a virtual professional profile and resume, but it provides a tremendous platform to celebrate your accomplishments, share and receive industry-specific information, develop referrals and endorsements, and provide an awesome avenue to connect with over 400 million people, in and out of your chosen profession. Within a matter of minutes you can create your LinkedIn profile and begin inviting others to connect with you.

One of the many benefits to a strong LinkedIn presence is its messaging system. You can send and receive messages to and from people in and out of your network. At first glance this may not seem like a big deal. However, people are far more likely to open, read and respond to a LinkedIn message than a standard email. If you are trying to become employed in the banking industry, but don't know anyone in banking, LinkedIn affords the opportunity to meet and develop relationships with people already working in it. Once you have one relationship established, you can request that connection to introduce you to others in their network. This applies to all industries (not just banking): Education, Health Care, Food Service, etc.

Companies regularly search LinkedIn profiles in an effort to recruit talent for positions they are trying to fill. They will search by education, experience and skill sets. LinkedIn also will notify you of job openings available for positions that require someone of your background and experience. I have received many paid invitations to speak from people I am connected with on LinkedIn. I recently opened a message from an elementary school principal who saw me speak at a conference a few years prior and had lost my contact information. She wanted me to do some professional development work with her faculty and was able to quickly find me through her LinkedIn account and reconnect with me.

Another great feature about LinkedIn is its amazing presence in search engines. If a company or hiring manager were to search your name, it is highly probable your LinkedIn profile would be one of the first links to pop up. Since most companies now search potential candidates to see who they really are, it's important that your search presence portrays you in the best light. Your LinkedIn profile can ensure this happens. They even have a feature now that allows you to transform your profile into your own web page.

If you don't have a LinkedIn account, go ahead and create one NOW! If you already have an account established, it would be a good idea to develop and strengthen your profile with the tips provided below and expand your network. Be sure to send me an invitation to connect and message with some feedback on this book!

Tips for a powerful LinkedIn profile, network and engagement:

- Remember, LinkedIn is a professional networking site! Keep everything you post, like or share professional! It isn't the platform for wedding, baby, vacation pics and random thoughts. Avoid engaging in controversial material that doesn't further or benefit yourself and everyone professionally.

- Post and share articles and other information relative to your industry and topics which may be important or trending in your profession.

- Your profile pic should be chosen very carefully. Selfies and vacation pics are a definite NO! It is worth the investment to have a professional headshot done to use as your profile picture. If you can't afford a professional photographer, then get a friend or an associate to take it. I am currently using a picture for my profile that a photographer took while I was speaking at an event. I especially like it because it captures me doing what I do and allows others viewing my profile to see me in action.

- Just like a resume, you want to update your profile information often. Any awards, certifications, or position changes should be added to your profile as they occur. Past positions should be written in past tense and present positions in present tense.

- Be sure to endorse others and serve as a reference for people in your network.

- Join LinkedIn groups relevant to your profession and be sure to engage and contribute to the group. If someone posts or publishes an article you benefit from, then it is important for you to like it, comment and share it. Others appreciate it when you show appreciation for their contributions.

- Research additional resources beyond this book that help develop and strengthen your LinkedIn profile.

...you have to GIVE in order to GET...

One of the best ways to meet influential people is by getting involved in volunteer, community and civic service. The most successful people I know are involved in giving their time, treasure and talent to causes they are passionate about. They don't get involved to receive any personal benefit, but rather they see the need and want to give back out of gratitude for what they have. Engaging in worthy causes affords you an opportunity to meet and work with others who also share the belief that those with so much have a duty to support those less fortunate.

I recently was asked to speak at an awards dinner for Boys and Girls Clubs; an organization to which I donate my time, treasure and talent. As a young person, I was a beneficiary of the programs provided by this great organization and those who contribute to it. It was my honor and privilege to speak at their Youth of the Year competition. Though I didn't know anyone personally in attendance at the banquet, I knew it was packed with people who volunteered their resources to make a difference in the lives of children. After the dinner I was approached by the mayor of the city, a CEO of a pharmacy and the director of a call center for a major mobile network provider. All three wanted me to speak and share with their employees. Had I not volunteered my time and given to a cause greater than myself, I wouldn't have had the opportunity to meet and connect with these people. Get involved in your local community, and get prepared for doors of opportunity to open your way.

...Look for ways to create opportunities and stand out...

While speaking on the campus of a well-known university, I met a student who exhibited the benefits of networking and the importance of staying vigilant in pursuit of opportunities. I remember this vividly, because upon arriving on campus the first building I pulled up to had a line of people waiting to get in. I remember getting a little nervous and equally excited about speaking to a crowd this large. It was hard to imagine thousands of people lined up to hear what I had to say. I lowered my window and asked the security guard directing traffic if I was at the University Center. He said, "No. The University Center is on the other side of campus." Disappointed that the crowd was not there to see me, I asked, "What's going on here? He said, "These people are all here to see Chuck Norris. He's speaking here tonight!" I raised the window and drove to the other end of campus where there were only a handful of students attending my presentation. Chuck Norris – 1, Brooks Harper – 0. It's not over yet!

During my presentation I asked for a show of hands of how many people had their resumes with them. No hands went up. I asked, "Why not?" I was about to launch into my point about how important it is to always have your resume with you because you never know who you're meeting, when a hand went up in the audience. I acknowledged him, and he said, "I don't have my resume but I have this…" He then handed me a business card with his name, phone number, email address, field of study, and career interests on it. I had never seen this concept before from a college student and asked him how he came up with the idea. He told me that as a student he attended a university function where a large number of business professionals had gathered. One of the business professionals there wanted to stay in touch with him and asked him for his business card. The problem was he didn't have a business card. Embarrassed, he decided to never to let that happen again. He went to his dorm room that night and used his laptop and printer to design his own business cards. He never wanted to miss another opportunity.

I asked the group I was speaking to if anyone else had a similar business card. No one did. I then asked if they could see the benefit of using a tool like this and how it might potentially set them apart from other people. They agreed that it would. I kept the card so I could stay in touch with him. I had no doubt in my mind that this sophomore was headed for greatness.

Don't limit yourself to contacts you already know. Keep in mind that everyone you come in contact with can become a member of your network. This includes people you have worked with at prior companies. I once re-interviewed with a company where I had been employed previously. My former manager was being promoted and referred me as a candidate for her position. The company initiating the contact didn't make the interview process any easier. Prior to interviewing, I had to do a series of online personality assessments and business acumen tests. After three interviews with various managers, the fourth interview was with the Regional Vice President. This interview was a breeze. We had worked together for a different company years earlier, and we sat there and swapped old stories from the past. At the end of the interview I learned, to my surprise, that he was not the final decision maker. He told me the final step would be flying to the corporate office, meeting with a psychologist, and interviewing with three members of the corporate executive management team.

I flew to the corporate office and was greeted by the impressive Executive Assistant to the Vice President of Sales and Marketing. She laid out the itinerary for the day and was a gracious host. I met with the psychologist for three hours. I answered a series of questions that included, "Have you ever told a lie to get out of trouble?" and "Did you ever steal anything when you were a child?"

After meeting with the psychologist, I met with three different vice presidents for about an hour each. All of the conversations went well. I flew home late that afternoon. On the flight home I was sitting beside a gentleman wearing flip flops reading the Wall Street Journal. He was amused as I told him about the interview process I had been through. I was equally amused when he told me he was the CEO of his company. He was impressed by the interview I had been on and the manner in which I conducted myself. We exchanged information, and he became one of my "contacts." After I arrived safely home, I sent him an email with my resume attached asking him to keep me in mind if he was looking for someone in the southeast market. He assured me he would. Every person you come in contact with is someone who can be added to your network. Granted, you don't have time to stay in touch with everyone you meet and cultivate every relationship, but planting seeds can often produce tremendous fruit at a later date. For the sake of time, be selective about which relationships you choose to invest in developing.

Two days after I arrived home from interviewing, the hiring manager called and said things went well with the psychologist. What a relief! She added that the corporate leadership team was very impressed, and they wanted to make me a formal offer for the position. The next day I received a formal six figure offer in writing along with the benefits package. After much consideration and to the company's surprise, I chose not to accept. One psychologist and seven interviews later, the company had forgotten to do one thing: sell me on why I should go back to work for them. Many companies are so selective in their interview process, that they forget the candidates they're hiring are also making decisions about being a part of their team. Be careful not to sell yourself short by taking the first great offer that comes along. A great financial offer doesn't always mean that it's the best job for you.

Developing a list of contacts and utilizing them can be essential in breaking through the front lines of an organization to get to the people making hiring decisions. Don't be embarrassed or too proud to reach out to friends and associates for leads on potential opportunities. If you end up being hired by a particular company, the person who referred you may be the beneficiary of a referral fee. Many companies offer incentives to their employees to refer candidates for open positions. The best form of repayment, to the contact who gets you in the door, is to be the best employee you can be and perform to the best of your abilities.

POTENTIAL CURVE BALL

"What's my receptionist's name?" Don't be surprised if you get this question. For many companies the receptionist is the "glue" of the entire organization and an essential part of the team. Their opinions are highly valued, and they are definitely part of the interview process. If you struggle to remember names, write them down, but whatever you do, don't forget them. In fact, it would be a nice gesture to take a proactive approach by commenting to the interviewer how professional and pleasant the receptionist was. Just, make sure you use this individual's name!

Action Items and Reminders from Chapter 2

1) Interviewing is a *contact* sport.

2) Make a list of personal and professional contacts who may be able to help you get an interview with their company.

3) Create or enhance your LinkedIn profile at www.linkedin.com. Send me an invitation to connect.

4) Get involved with at least one organization that allows you to share your time, treasure and talents.

5) Look for and consider ways to make yourself stand out.

6) Helping people in your network strengthens those relationships.

7) Keep your resume with you and updated at all times.

8) If you don't already have a business card, create one.

Chapter 3
Who's interviewing who?

From the time you sent in your resume or application, the interview started. Let's assume that your resume made it to the human resources department and was selected along with twenty others for a screening interview. You get the call from HR asking to set up a time for some short phone screening questions. You say, "Let me look at my calendar," and a date is set. During your screening interview you blast the questions out of the park, and then you ask how you did. They confirm that they liked what they heard, and you proceed to ask what the next step is. They tell you they are bringing four people in for face-to-face interviews; if you are one of the four, they will call and let you know. You use what you have learned thus far to articulate a beautiful pitch for why you should be one of the four candidates to be interviewed face-to-face. **(Don't forget to have your calendar handy to confirm your availability for their available dates.)** Your date is confirmed, and you are ready to close the deal. Be warned that every step you take moving forward will be critical to getting the offer. This is where details become very important.

POTENTIAL CURVE BALL

It is not uncommon for hiring managers to ask to see your calendar during the interview. They are looking to see how well you plan and organize. If they don't see anything in your calendar, they may assume you don't even use your calendar. If you use your computer to schedule and plan, then print out three months' worth and have them with you.

...You are always interviewing...

This statement may seem a bit elementary, but be sure to have your suit pressed, shoes polished, hair done, nails clipped, teeth brushed and mints in your pocket. Take a couple of extra copies of your resume, a small notepad, a pen and your calendar. I was recently eating breakfast in a restaurant while working on this book, and the manager came over and asked me what I was working on. I told him about this book and some of the concepts I outline in it. He shared with me that one of the things that tips him off that someone isn't a good candidate is if they ask for a pen to fill out the application. That tells him they are not prepared.

When you arrive for the interview, make sure you park in designated parking. I suggest arriving 30 minutes early in order to collect all items you are taking in and get your thoughts together. You don't want to have to go back out to your car to get something you have forgotten. Remember, you are always interviewing and every interaction you have with anyone is part of that interview, so don't take anything for granted. You also don't want to be too relaxed. You want to strike the right balance of being on your toes, but not so tense that you lose your personality. When you arrive be friendly, smile, and let the receptionist or greeter know who you are there to see. Stay professional, but keep it conversational. You are simply there to tell your story.

Make sure you give a firm handshake. I always squeeze the person's hand to the exact pressure that they are squeezing mine. This applies to both males and females. If you are fortunate to be interviewed in the hiring manager's office, look for personal belongings (pictures, diplomas, sports memorabilia, etc.) that may tell you a little bit about the person. Commenting on something you see can help break the ice. (See my response to "What's the last book you read?" in Chapter 4 for an example of breaking the ice.) Let me reiterate, there is such a thing as getting too relaxed in the interview. You want to maintain your professionalism at all times, taking nothing for granted and always appearing confident but not arrogant:

Interviewer: What type of experience do you have?

Lumberjack: Have you ever heard of the Sahara Forest?

Interviewer: NO, I have heard of the Sahara DESERT.

Lumberjack: Well, that's what they call it now!

...who's interviewing who???

Interviews typically start with an overview of your resume or application. Depending upon the persons conducting the interview, discussion of your resume and relevant work experience may start at the bottom or the top. Once you see their starting point, this is an opportunity to assert yourself and guide the interview for a moment--if they let you. If they start at the bottom of your work experience, go ahead and take the liberty of walking them through the rest of your resume. In order to do this, you will need to know your resume like the back of your hand. Highlight any accomplishments and promotions along the way, and smoothly transition from one position to the next. Controlling the narrative allows you to side-step potential land mines on your resume. Gaps in employment, switching to competitors and low GPA can all be things that raise red flags on your resume and could be highlighted by your interviewer. Companies always want to know why you left your previous positions and why you are looking to leave your current situation. Taking a proactive approach and being prepared to give a logical explanation in a strong and confident manner will quickly make any red flag a non-issue.

I never bring up my college GPA, because it is not particularly impressive. On the occasions when I am asked about it, I give this response:

> "During my first two years of college I was not as attentive to my studies as I should have been. However, during my junior and senior years I moved into my

major, buckled down and truly began to pour everything into my classes. As a result, my grades improved dramatically. I would like for you to focus on my GPA while I was in my major; it is more indicative of my current work ethic and the person I am today."

Without exception, this response has always diffused this potential land mine and softened what could have been a rough spot in the interview process.

The stories that I tell in interviews have proven to work well, and your stories will be no exception. But without documented proof, the stories you are telling are just that: stories. I never go on an interview without my credibility binder. The pharmaceutical industry calls it a brag book, academia calls it "vita," and in the art world it's a "portfolio." It is a compilation of your work, awards, certificates, "pat on the back" notes and emails, rankings, etc., neatly placed in plastic sleeves in a three ring leather binder, offering documentation that everything you are saying in your interview is true and accurate. Place everything in your binder in chronological order with your resume, from the beginning of your career to the present. It is not sophomoric to include extraordinary accomplishments from high school and earlier, as this shows an even longer history of excellence in your life. If you were an Eagle Scout or President of a student organizations like Future Business Leaders of America or Future Farmers of America, put it in there! By placing things in chronological order, you can easily reference documentation as needed.

Imagine you are walking the interviewer through your resume, and you get to a point where you highlight one of your accomplishments from your current or past positions. Simultaneously you open your credibility binder, and right there at your fingertips is an email from one of your managers, thanking you for an outstanding job on that project. It's true that facts tell and stories sell, but documented stories are even more powerful. Now the person interviewing you has documented proof that what you are telling them is true. This gives you credibility and relieves anxiety for them. It will also set you apart from everyone else who is interviewing for the position. I had to learn this the hard way.

I heard for years that you should never go on an interview without a professional credibility binder. So I spent a good amount of energy putting together a slick marketing portfolio of my career, only to be disappointed when no one ever asked to see it. I have taken my credibility binder on countless interviews and no one has ever asked to see it. It finally dawned on me that it was not their responsibility to ask to see documentation of my success; it was my responsibility to show them. The burden of proof is on the person being interviewed. After this revelation, I began to proactively show results for what I have done, using my credibility binder while simultaneously walking them through my resume and during the Q&A portion of the interview. Incorporating this practice into my interviews has increased my offer rate tremendously for a couple of reasons: 1) Done properly, it portrays you as an honest, competent professional and 2) Many have a brag book, but very few are proactively using it as they answer interview questions. Since interviewers rarely ask to see it, chances are they won't. Proactively sharing your brag book with interviewers gives you a distinct competitive advantage over every other candidate and sets you apart.

Once you have completed the narrative of your resume, pause to allow the person interviewing you the opportunity to take back control of the interview. At this point, interviewers will more than likely transition into their prepared questions. The next chapter will address typical questions asked, why they are asked and how to respond to each.

Typically when interviewers are through with their questions, you will be given an opportunity to ask questions of your own. **Note: If they don't offer the opportunity for you to ask questions, then ask for the opportunity to ask questions.** This is a pivotal stage in the interview. It is an opportunity for you to shine, and it allows them a chance to see how you perform when the roles are reversed.

The questions you ask can be as important as your answers to their questions. Your questions, and the manner in which you ask them, demonstrate how you conduct yourself when you are in the driver's seat. You now are able to showcase your level of interest in the position and give them the opportunity to sell you on why you should come to work for them. Conducted properly, this portion of the interview can close the deal and position you as the top candidate of choice. Asking genuine, compelling questions can plant a seed in interviewers' minds that they must convince you their company should be your employer of choice. Psychologically, their role changes from interviewers to recruiters. Being recruited is much more fun than being a job seeker. Once this transformation takes place, it is common for your interviewers to begin telling and selling all the other decision makers on why they think you would be the best candidate for the position.

The following are some of the questions I like to ask potential employers:

Do you feel I would be a good candidate for this position?

This question could knock them a little out of their comfort zone, but their response should give you a good indication of how you did on your interview. Even if they give you a textbook, corporate answer, look for clues in their facial expressions and body language. Smiling is definitely a good sign. If their response to this question doesn't reveal any concerns they may have with hiring you, follow up with the next question.

Do you have any reservations or concerns about hiring me?

Depending on the company and the individual, the person conducting the interview may open up and tell you some concerns regarding your potential hire. If a concern is mentioned, it is essential that you address it properly. I use a technique I learned called "EAR," which stands for empathize, ask, and respond. This technique takes some practice, but used properly can overcome just about any objection. Your initial response should be to acknowledge their concern as legitimate. Suppose the company you are interviewing with shares their concern with your lack of experience. An example of an empathy statement could be: "I can understand/appreciate why my lack of experience could be a concern for you." The next step is to ask a clarification question that shows you truly understand their concern and would like to know a little more. An appropriate clarification question could be: "Has a lack of experience been an issue with people you have hired in the past?" You then wait for their clarification before responding to their concern. You then articulate a response that offers reassurance their concern will not be an issue if you are fortunate enough to be the candidate of choice. If it is a concern of lack of experience, you may highlight some of your life experience that is relevant to the work experience they require. Often when concerns surface, there is a natural tendency for one to become defensive. If you become defensive in the interview, it could be an indicator that you are not open to coaching or constructive criticism, and could be difficult to lead and manage. By using the "EAR" technique, you will simultaneously diffuse their concerns and show you are indeed coachable and willing to accept constructive feedback.

What do you enjoy about working here?

This gives the persons interviewing you a chance to highlight the positive things about their company. They may even open up a little more about themselves and their successes. Receive what is said with equal enthusiasm. Their response could lead to additional follow-up questions or an opportunity for you to respond with something like: "I hope to enjoy that same type of success and career fulfillment here!"

How soon are you planning to fill this position?

Knowing when the position is to be filled gives you an indication as to how far along they are in the decision process. Sometimes the answers you get are vague, and sometimes estimated hire dates are moved based on budgets or a variety of factors. If you detect a sense of urgency about filling the open position, this could be a good sign for you. Unfortunately, some companies are constantly interviewing candidates even though they are not actually planning to hire anyone at that particular time. The philosophy behind this workforce strategy is to constantly have a fresh pool of qualified applicants in the event a position becomes available. It is a savvy, proactive practice on the part of the company, but can be extremely frustrating for someone who needs employment now! I have been on both sides of the equation as a job seeker and hiring manager. As a manager, I would let applicants know the timeline for hiring decisions whether they asked or not out of courtesy. As a job seeker, a great interview can get your hopes up about a new exciting opportunity only to end up being a huge disappointment if you learn there is not an actual position currently available. I prefer to know their timeline, especially if I am interviewing with more than one company or considering multiple offers.

(JUGGLING MULTIPLE OFFERS)

Juggling multiple offers can indeed be a circus act. While receiving an offer that puts a paycheck in your bank account and food on your table, you may simultaneously be only halfway through the interview process with a more preferable company or waiting on a pending offer. This can be a very tricky situation. What if you accept the current offer and then receive the more preferred offer two weeks later? Or, what if you decline the current offer in hopes the other opportunity works out, but it doesn't?

This is where it helps to have a career coach to bounce these predicaments off of and get advice. Every situation is different, and this can be very difficult to navigate. I once worked with a client who accepted a position and two weeks later, while he was away at orientation training, was offered a better opportunity. Together we kicked around the opportunities from every angle. He decided to accept the second offer, humbly resign and fly back home. It was an extremely difficult decision, but one he felt was the best for him in the long run. You may be faced with these decisions throughout your career. Surround yourself with solid people whose advice you value and trust. Weighing both the short and long-term impact, make the decision that is in your best interest and always be professional and courteous to everyone along the way.

If I am fortunate enough to get this position, to whom would I be reporting?

I always like to know who I am going to be working for and whether or not I feel we are compatible. When I am interviewing with a person who could potentially be my manager, I am deciding if I can envision myself working for that person and enjoying it. Sometimes the hiring manager will be excited about you, but you aren't getting the same warm and fuzzy feeling. If this is the case, think long and hard before you accept the position. It can be better to wait for the right boss to come along. It may be you will have to report to multiple managers, which can add a whole other degree of difficulty and stress to a position. Many variables should be considered when accepting an offer. Chapter 6 will discuss offer acceptance in greater detail.

When your time is done and you have answered their questions and asked yours, then thank them for their time and let them know you are looking forward to speaking with them again soon. Ask for their business cards or contact information so you can follow up with them. Stay professional the entire time you are on the property and be cordial to everyone you come in contact with, including other candidates who are interviewing. I once interviewed for a position where the company had every candidate for the position stand and give a 3-minute presentation in front of the entire pool of candidates. When everyone was finished, we each had to write down on a sheet of paper the reason we thought we were the best candidate for the position, and the one person we would hire besides ourselves. The hiring manager took into account the votes from the other candidates when making his decision. I know this because, not only did I receive the most votes from everyone else, but I was offered and accepted the position.

When interviewing for a position, remember that it is your responsibility to interview the company and hiring manager as well. Done properly it will enhance your candidacy and give you the information you need to make your decision. Be sure to send a handwritten thank you card and email to everyone pertinent to the hiring decision with whom you came into contact. This is a professional courtesy and shows your appreciation for their time and consideration.

POTENTIAL CURVE BALL

I worked as a hiring manager for a publicly-traded company shortly after graduating from college. We hired the best and brightest college graduates for our Manager Trainee Program. A potential candidate would go through 4 or 5 interviews ending with a final sit-down with the Regional Vice President (RVP.) We once had a candidate who was approaching the final step in the interview process. The coaching he received from us was to go in and have a simple conversation with the RVP and not blow it. Well…He blew it, but not how you think. Twenty minutes after the interview started, the RVP came out and said we couldn't hire him. We were in shock. When we asked for his reasoning, he told us that our candidate had left the small second buttons on his shirtsleeve unbuttoned. The RVP said this was an indicator that our candidate lacked attention to detail. He said, "We need people who can get the decimal point in the right place, get the "i's" dotted and the "t's" crossed, and he isn't that person." Unfortunately, there was nothing we could do.

Action Items and Reminders from Chapter 3

1) Proactively walk the interviewer through your resume.

2) Develop a professional credibility binder, packed with awards, certificates, eye-popping reports, etc. that document your successes.

3) Practice incorporating your credibility binder into your answers.

4) Make a list of compelling questions to ask.

5) Have an interview coach or someone you can get advice from during the process.

6) Follow up in writing.

Chapter 4

They've Got Questions, You've Got Answers!

I remember courses in college that allowed the use of textbooks during exams. These always seemed to be the hardest exams to take. When some people hear "open book test", they automatically assume no study is required. Their strategy is to look up the answers in the book on test day. The problem with this method is those exams typically are deliberately longer and more difficult. Relying solely on the book to answer every question would allow only enough time to complete approximately 20% of the exam. Interviewing is not any different. Even if you know the questions and the answers, you still have to set aside time to prepare and practice. This chapter will cover questions you are likely to encounter in an interview. It won't do you any good if you do not take the time to prepare responses and practice delivering them.

...interviewing is an open book test...

Working as a speaker and trainer with a large corporation, I had to memorize lengthy scripts of speeches. There was a point in my tenure with this company when I had six different 45-minute scripts committed to memory. That is a lot of information to recall and deliver fluidly with more than 95% accuracy. I was able to do this because I didn't just sit down and memorize the information. I would actually stand up and practice delivering the speech as if an audience of 500 people was in front of me. Actually speaking the words helped me take the information from my mind and move it across my lips. This allowed me to notice which portions of the script would cause me trouble in delivering. Whenever I reached a point that tripped me up, I would practice saying that part over and over. Words like "participative" and "communicative" began to roll right off of my tongue with ease. What looked easy to my audience was a result of a relentless pursuit of excellence through rigorous practice. When a professional golfer hits a ball, he makes it look easy. What the viewing audience doesn't see are the hundreds of balls he put in the woods while practicing. Practicing the telling of your stories to answer interview questions should involve the same preparation and commitment.

In Chapter One we talked about the ability to tell your story as you answer questions. This chapter will discuss examples of the questions asked in interviews and the motives behind them. Understanding why a certain question is asked will better prepare you to answer it. Sometimes the motive is not so you can give them a great reason to hire you, but an attempt to reveal a reason why you should **not** be hired. I call these "gotcha" questions. They are designed to reveal certain characteristics about you, which, if perceived as negative, could raise red flags and cost you the opportunity to work at a particular company.

Solid companies with human resources departments typically have a standard set of questions they ask every person interviewed. It is important for them to ask everyone the same questions to be consistent and to eliminate bias in the interview process. This chapter will cover some of the most popular questions employers ask, the motives behind the questions, and examples of approaches you may want to take with these types of questions. Though your answers may be different from mine, the explanations offered will provide you a foundation to build and articulate your compelling responses.

Tell me a little about yourself? (2-minute commercial)

This question is often referred to as the 2-minute commercial or elevator speech. If you're ever riding on an elevator with someone influential, you would want to have a mini-infomercial ready that explains who you are and what you are all about, just in case you ever got your break. It is an open-ended question that allows you to talk about yourself, and normally is asked early on in the interview. Though it is like an infomercial, it should not sound like one.

This question gives you an opportunity at the beginning of the interview to capture their interest and get the company excited about you and wanting to learn more. You will tell them what type of person you are, characteristics that describe you, and your interests. With this question, as well as any others, avoid any negative statements about yourself. Don't beat yourself up. It's the company's job to uncover the areas in which you are challenged. Don't list any reasons they shouldn't hire you. This may sound like common sense, but you would be surprised at the number of people who reveal a negative self-image in the first question. You don't want the interview to be over before it starts.

Keep your response short, concise and powerful. Don't go on and on about yourself for 15 minutes, but don't sell yourself short with a 5-second response either. Writing in advance and delivering it aloud is strongly suggested. Record yourself delivering it, and play it back.

Why are you interested in working for our organization?

This question will reveal several things about you to the company with whom you are interviewing. It will tell them your motive for selecting their organization to be your employer, and how passionate you are about being a part of their team. It will also reveal how much you know about their company, and how well you prepared will demonstrate your level of interest. Job seekers who possess a strong desire to work for a particular organization typically have a good reason for doing so. If the company is selective and exclusive, the reality is everyone wants to work for them. Part of your preparation for the interview will be to find out everything you can about the organization. Much of this information can be found on the company's website or other places on the internet. Your research will include finding the company's mission, vision, and values statements. Your answer to "Why are you interested in working for our organization?" may include a statement that shows how your personal value system is compatible with their company in terms of integrity, character, and quality. You're not going to tell them that you want to work there because of all the vacation and sick time they provide their employees. You may comment on how long the company has been in business and that you also think long-term and want a lasting career with them.

You will need to look beyond the first page of their website to get a clear picture of what the company is all about. When I interview with a publicly traded company, I listen to the webcast of their quarterly shareholders' meeting. These meetings are recorded and often posted on the investors' page of the company's website. They usually feature the executive management team reporting on the health and wealth of the company. Analysts ask them the tough questions which reveal the true stability of the company, as well as the items that are crucial to their business and industry. For example, you may learn from a webcast that the company is heading in a new direction, or launching a new product or service. It may be that you have a particular knowledge, skill or ability that would be beneficial to the company in that particular area. Knowing this, you may respond with a statement such as this: "I am especially excited about the company branching out into Europe. Since we are in a global economy, it is important to conduct business both domestically and abroad. My family was stationed in Germany for 10 years, and I am extremely familiar with their culture." Chances are that no one else interviewing this day has bothered to listen to the webcast and has no clue about the future direction of the company. Your preparation has positioned you to appear extremely knowledgeable of the organization's priorities, lending credibility to your true motive for wanting to be a part of their team.

...Be Knowledgeable, but not a "Know-it-All"...

You have to be careful not to appear to be a know-it-all. Remember that you are still on the outside looking in. If you are perceived as overconfident and cocky, then the hiring team may be concerned with how receptive you will be to coaching and constructive criticism. I have a friend who was somewhat of an overachiever. When she began the interviewing process after college, she researched a particular company to the point that she knew more about it than her interviewer. In fact, at one point during the interview she corrected the person on a statement he made. She called me after the interview, and told me that she may have overdone it. It's acceptable to learn as much as you can about a company, but you don't want to embarrass the person for whom you may be working.

Why have you chosen this particular field?

This question is asked to find out if the position for which you are interviewing is truly a good "fit" for you. Human resources managers are very aware that not everyone who applies for a position plans to stay with their company. They want to make sure you're not just looking for something to hold you over until your next opportunity comes along. Turnover is extremely expensive, and, by hiring the right people the first time, companies keep their costs down and are more productive. Your response should include specific characteristics about yourself which affirm that the position for which you are applying is a natural fit for you. This is a good place to tell a story about yourself. It may be a funny story from your childhood that made such an impression on your life, you knew beyond a shadow of a doubt you were born to do this. A strong, compelling story at this juncture in the interview will continue to drive a deeper wedge between you and the rest of the field of candidates.

What are your strengths?

This question could be a total setup. What do I mean? You have already revealed some of the strengths you have at this point. You discussed your passions and why you chose this field based on your characteristics and skills. Interviewers **have** to ask you this question, to get to the question they really want to ask you, which is coming next. You need to give some concrete statements on your strengths, based on the things you know they are looking for in a candidate, for instance: energetic, detail-oriented, integrity, communication, etc. Of course you need to slide a few adjectives in front of those strengths: "I have impeccable integrity; I am an effective communicator both orally and written; and I have tireless energy." Choose the words you use to describe yourself carefully. It doesn't hurt to throw in some color and flair. The truth is we all have certain areas wherein we excel. Knowing what you are really exceptional at is important, because it will be those strengths that help outweigh the areas in which you are weaker or more challenged. If you do an awesome job of presenting your strengths, your deficiencies are less of a factor.

What are your weaknesses?

My answer to this question has evolved over the years. The question itself still remains quite frustrating at times, because what we hear is, "Why shouldn't we hire you?" It makes it seem like asking about your strengths is more like a setup question to ask about your shortcomings. But that is the wrong attitude to have toward this question. It is important for the company interviewing you to know the areas in which you require improvement, so they can make the most out of your orientation and training period once you are hired.

My previous advice would have been to answer this question with a clever way of turning your weaknesses into a positive such as: "I have a tendency to take on too much responsibility". The strategy here was to send an underlying message that you are an extremely hard worker. This approach is tired, washed out and over with. It is limiting in its impact, and I doubt it ever satisfied its intent or truthfully answered the question. If you answer this question in this manner, you will sound like everyone else and totally miss an awesome opportunity to differentiate yourself.

I now propose an entirely different approach that is bold and refreshing: BE COMPLETELY FORTHCOMING AND TRANSPARENT. Go ahead and tell them the areas you are challenged in. That's right! If you aren't detailed-oriented, tell them. If you struggle staying organized, let them know. They are going to find out eventually when you are hired. You don't want to be the new employee with damaged credibility two weeks into the position because you fudged an interview question.

So tell them your "weaknesses", but make sure you include this critical addition: explain what you are doing to overcome or compensate for your weaknesses. Show them you are proactive and solutions oriented by sharing the books you've read, the training courses you have taken, and the tools and techniques you have acquired to improve your skill in this area.

By openly sharing your areas of challenge and the steps you have climbed to overcome them, you establish integrity and display your willingness to invest in your own personal and professional development. Companies want to know that you are interested in growing, developing and willing to do what is necessary to perform at your best.

This is the most effective way to turn a weakness into a strength.

Describe your best/worst boss.

Both of these can be gotcha questions, especially if you liked your best boss because he let you come in late and leave early. The best boss I ever had challenged and supported my efforts and viewed my success as his success. We had robust dialogue, and I was held accountable to perform and rewarded for victories.

Describing the worst boss you ever had can be a little tricky, especially if the people interviewing you have some of the same characteristics. Of course, if that is the case then you probably don't want to work for them anyway. You want to exercise caution with your response. If you are not careful, you can appear to be the type of person who is difficult to manage, insubordinate or confrontational. When many people are faced with this question, it forces them to relive some potentially painful work experiences which may produce emotion if not properly harnessed. I once interviewed someone whose entire demeanor changed when asked this question. It pushed this person's button, and he then proceeded to share for the next five minutes how much the former manager was detested. Before this person knew what happened, total cohesion was lost, which affected the rest of the interview. Don't fall victim to this.

I generally use the following response: "During my career I have been fortunate to work for some extremely talented managers. They were effective coaches and motivated me to perform beyond expectations. I could contact anyone of them right now and get a glowing recommendation, if needed, for a reference. I haven't really had a terrible boss, but I once had an executive level manager whom I did not hold in high regard. He had a tendency to lecture as opposed to coach. His visits typically highlighted things that were wrong with very little emphasis on the positives." Most hiring managers will empathize with this situation. In this response, I'm not throwing my previous managers under the bus, but I am answering the question without raising a serious red flag. If you try to duck this question by saying you have never had a boss you didn't care for, they won't buy it.

Where do you see yourself in 3-5 years?

This question is asked to reveal your ambition, aspirations, and goal setting ability. It is surprising the number of people who do not set realistic career goals for themselves. If you don't have at least a general goal for the next 3-5 years, then the person interviewing you is going to assume that you are simply desperate for a job or not forward thinking.

I asked someone this question once when I first became a manager, and he told me he always wanted to be a police officer. I really liked the individual and knew he would be successful in the position for which I was hiring, so I brought him on board. He was a great employee, but a year later he resigned to pursue his dream of being a police officer. Shortly thereafter I was interviewing someone who gave me the same response as my former employee. I asked him, "What are you doing here? Go be a police officer!" I learned my lesson: Don't hire someone who wants to be something else. They will never be satisfied until they pursue their dream.

Your response to this question should include that in the next 3-5 years you plan to still be working for their company. In addition, your 3-5 year goal should display your ambition, energy, and drive to grow with the company through promotion, or at least professional development. This is also a question where you can insert some of the information you gleaned during your research on the company. Perhaps you uncovered that the company spends 10% of its gross sales in research and development of new products and services. You could tell them how excited you are that their company sees the benefit of investing in the future through R&D, and that a decision to hire you is an extension of this type of investment. You have the same career philosophy they do: You want to grow and develop as a professional. You believe their company provides the perfect opportunity to fulfill that goal.

Describe yourself with one word.

How can anyone possibly describe themselves in one word? This request is similar to, "If you could be any animal in the world, what would it be and why?" Although it can be difficult to summarize yourself with one word, it is asked with consistency in many interviews. People offer words like: energetic, honest, resourceful, etc. These are the same generic words that they put on their resume, echoed in the two minute drill and probably used in the last question, "Why should we hire you?" It's repetitive, boring, and has low-impact. If you are asked to provide a word, make it one that sums up all of these things and be ready to explain it. By the way, don't simply tell them the word that describes you best and then wait on the next question. State the word and then give a simple, brief explanation. When I am asked to describe myself in one word I have responded with: "appropriate." That's right! "Appropriate." I then explain that whatever situation I am in, I conduct myself appropriately using discernment and common sense. It sets me apart from everyone else who uses the same old, tired buzz words.

What was the last book you read?

Companies are interested in how much initiative you take in your own professional development. Reading books and publications is highly thought of by hiring managers. It shows that you take a personal interest in advancing your career, and you are motivated to invest your own resources to get where you want to be. I agree that the last three books a person reads reveals a lot about who they are at work and at home. It so happens that I enjoy reading financial and motivational books. These types of books are viewed favorably by many hiring managers, who also read them. This question resurfaces often in my interviews. In most cases the books I had read were impressive, but not every time. Ironically, I was interviewing with a publishing company once, and they inquired of the last book I had read. It so happened that the last book I had read was a politically charged book. The disposition of the person interviewing me changed completely. In that instance I knew that because I had read that particular book, he immediately associated me with the political views of the writer. Whether I agreed with the author or not, I had made a classic blunder. Bringing up politics in an interview, intentionally or not, can be divisive. I got a voicemail from him later letting me know they had chosen another candidate. Even some of Tom Brady's passes hit the ground on Sunday.

I was preparing for an interview once with this particular question in mind. I had recently finished reading a short book entitled, "212 The Extra Degree" by Sam Parker and Mac Anderson.[1] It was a simple concept about going the extra degree to be the best you can be. Anticipating being asked the last book I had read, I decided to try a different approach. I thought it would be a bold gesture to give the hiring manager my copy of the book as a gift. I was a little hesitant because I wasn't sure if this person would be comfortable accepting a gift from a potential candidate, but I knew I had to do something to set myself apart. I walked into the interview, shook his hand and then slid the book across the table. I told him I had recently finished the book, and I hoped he would enjoy it as much as I had. He grinned so wide he could have eaten a banana sideways. He went on to tell me how he had just trained his entire team on the same concepts that were in the book. The ice was broken. From that point on he and I were simply having a conversation, which is exactly how I like it. Sometimes you have to take bold steps to stand out and set yourself apart from other candidates. Be prepared to discuss the last book you read and make it interesting.

What is your biggest professional accomplishment?

If you are a recent high school or college graduate, this question can be difficult to answer, because the reality is you haven't done that much yet. You went from high school straight to college and have had very few opportunities to accomplish much professionally. If this is your situation, hopefully you were involved in clubs and other organizations while in school that gave you a chance to achieve great things. Maybe you were in an internship program which afforded you the opportunity to work on and, perhaps even spearhead a new initiative. In the beginning of my career I often discussed senior projects from college for this portion of my interviews.

If you have been in the workforce for a while, then answering this question shouldn't be an issue. Think about that one great project or event you worked on that was a huge success and earned praise and applause from your manager. Hopefully you received a thank you in writing, in an email or an award for your efforts. This is a good place in the interview to open your credibility binder and show the documented recognition you received. Remember, documentation substantiates what you tell interviewers and visualizes the impact your work had on the organization.

How did you hear about this position?

Companies spend a large sum of money to establish their brand (who they are) and value proposition (what they do). They track the return on investment of their marketing dollars by calculating the cost to obtain a new customer, and the amount of money each spends. Similarly, companies spend a lot of cash to market themselves to the best talent available to employ. They want to be the employer of choice for the best and brightest career seekers. Just like tracking customers, companies also keep a sharp eye on how potential employees learn about them. Was it word of mouth, a referral, a job board, through a college or university?

Companies have egos! How you learned about the position in a company can signal to them not only the sincerity of your intent, but how highly you value the opportunity to work for them. If your pursuit of the current position you are interviewing for is random, it may deflate the way they feel about you. You could be seen as unserious or disingenuous. Whether it was random or you have been dreaming about the position for years, your answer should reflect your enthusiasm toward the opportunity and how much earning the spot truly means to you. In essence, this question presents an opportunity to stroke the ego of the company as well as an awesome chance to convince them why you are the best and only person for the job. Your answer will affirm what they already know to be true: This position is a unique and exciting opportunity for the person they hire. Your answer could go something like this:

> "When I learned about this position through _____ (Insert Source), I jumped at the opportunity to work with you. I appreciate the challenges this position provides, the importance of having the right person in it, and the potential to not only stretch myself, but to make an impact for your company. I am looking forward to bringing everything I have to this position, and I would be thrilled to be on your team."

Your answer fulfills their desire to know how you learned about the position, their need to feel great about their company, and also strengthens your candidacy.

What is your dream job?

Is this a trick question? Aren't you suppose to say the position you are interviewing for **is** your dream job? Sure, but only if it really is! If the position you are interviewing for is the one you've always wanted, then tell them how much it means to you and the value, energy and ambition you are planning to bring to make it reality. But if it isn't, then don't try and fake it, because they'll see right through you. This question is asked in an effort to gauge how interested you are in the current position and where you see it taking you. Companies will try and weed out candidates here who don't necessarily want the job or folks they view as too short term, who may potentially leave the position before they can recoup their investment in hiring and training them. It costs time and money each instance an employee is turned over. Instead, talk about how much working in the position you are interviewing for means to you and how it meets the long range goals you have for your career.

Know that if you are interviewing for a position such as assistant manager at a grocery store or restaurant and you tell them your dream job is to be a nurse, you may not get hired if you leave it there. Here's why: For starters, they may wonder why you aren't pursuing being a nurse already. It may plant the seed that you've tried to become a nurse, but no one has hired you, which opens another list of questions and concerns. Secondly, their concern will be you may leave the first chance you get to become a nurse.

Your answer, if this isn't your dream job, should offer reassurance that, even though it isn't the job you've always wanted, you are still 100% committed to the position and plan to make it worth their while if given the chance. You may consider adding a verbal commitment to stay for a minimum length of time, but only if you plan to fulfill the promise.

What other companies are you interviewing with?

This question could be a double-edged sword depending upon the philosophy of the company and/or person who is doing the interviewing. Let me explain. If the ego of the person or company who is interviewing you is inflated, they may take offence to someone interviewing with other companies. This is rarely the case, but know it may exist. More often than not, companies ask this question so they know who their competition is and how hard and fast they need to pursue you. Interviewing with other companies can make your candidacy appear more attractive and desirable, and create a sense of urgency in presenting you with an offer. Having multiple companies interested in you creates perceived demand for your services and could potentially impact the amount of money they're willing to pay to ensure you accept their offer. When I was interviewing with multiple companies, not being limited to one opportunity provided a huge confidence boost which helped me relax and not seem desperate. So there is certainly a psychological advantage to interviewing with other companies simultaneously. It also sends a message that you are a prudent person and not someone who puts all of their eggs in one basket.

Why are you leaving your current job?

There comes a time with almost every job when your relationship with the company or the position has run its course, and it's time to move on. Sometimes we stay too long, and other times we leave prematurely. One of the factors working in the favor of someone switching careers or companies is it's now expected. It is rare now for a person to stay with the same employer or in the same position for the duration of their 30 to 40 year career. Companies today are a bit more understanding of higher frequency changes, and they compete with each other to recruit and retain the best talent. This shouldn't be an encouragement to anyone to switch jobs every 6 months because it's now OK and expected, but it does make it a little easier to answer the question.

The great thing about this question is that it forces you to really think about why you want to change and whether or not this is the right move. I have worked with clients who sought interview coaching from me only to discover that what they thought was their dream job would have been a huge mistake. Sometimes through the arduous exploration of new horizons you discover how great the career you already have, and the company you're with, actually are; and that it was simply the lens by which you viewed your situation that needed to be adjusted.

If you are part of a workforce reduction or job elimination, answering this question is fairly easy. You explain the reason your present or previous company is restructuring and how this presents an exciting opportunity for both yourself and the company with which you are interviewing. It is more difficult and complicated to answer this question if you are looking for "a change", "something new" or "different", "a challenge", because you have to be able to explain why these things are not available at your current job or company. The company interviewing you will be trying to figure out whether or not the problem is you.

So the challenge is to answer in a positive manner, while simultaneously conveying your potential value, without seeming like a disgruntled, unmanageable, unappreciative burnout.

What type of work environment do you prefer?

This question is asked to determine whether or not you are a good fit for the company and/or position. The company may operate at an extremely fast pace, or the particular position may require painstaking, methodical research and thought. If they are looking for a "Steady Eddie" and you work like "Speedy Gonzales", then you're not the right person for the job. Both you and they would become frustrated very quickly in your tenure.

Some applicants and recruiters will avoid this question from time to time in an effort to fill a position out of expedience. Because they can discern your ability to do the job, they ignore the fact that you may not be happy, thus making your stay short-lived. If this question isn't asked, you should ask them about the work environment. There is no need to waste your time or theirs. You want to make sure the job is suitable and will allow you to thrive and perform at your best for as long as you need or desire.

What motivates you?

Co-Worker 1: How long have you worked here?
Co-Worker 2: Ever since they threatened to fire me!

Unfortunately many don't get in gear or perform at their best until threatened with disciplinary action or job loss. While it's true that great leaders light a fire **in** their employees while bosses only light a fire **under** their employees, it is incumbent upon you to be SELF-motivated. If your manager has to get you going every day to get you to perform at your best, or threaten you to get you to work on time, then you may be more trouble than you are worth. Being self-motivated means you don't have to be inspired by anyone else, but something inside of you drives you to perform at your best!

Is there a right answer to this question? Yes, but it can depend on the company and/or position they're trying to fill. They know some people are motivated by money; that their level of performance is closely tied to financial incentives such as commissions, bonuses, prizes and pay increases. Sales and marketing positions are often filled with people who are motivated in this manner. Other positions are less quantifiable and may require someone motivated by the opportunity the job offers to make a difference in the lives of others. Some people are motivated by work-life balance and the flexibility of the work schedule. More and more companies are using personality exams to uncover true motivation. Through a series of questions about things preferred, or not preferred, they attempt to peek inside and figure out what makes a person tick.

Personal motivators are things to examine and know about yourself as you prepare for your interview. During the interview is not the time for soul searching and thinking out loud through this question. Know yourself!

Gaps in employment?

This question should be answered before it's asked. When hiring managers look at your application, employment history is one of the first things they focus on. They're looking at where you worked, positions held, what you accomplished and over what time period. When there are significant gaps of time (3 months or more), it can signal you may be as inconsistent as your work history, so these gaps need to be accounted for and explained. A good time to do this is when you are telling them about yourself. When you address it proactively, it takes out the awkwardness, because you are answering it on your terms, and it relieves them of the obligation to ask. Once you cover this ground, it frees up you and them to focus on what really matters: your value and how they can benefit from hiring you. For example: "You will notice from February to August I wasn't employed. I left my position during this period to care for a sick loved one and went straight back to work! You'll also notice on my resume I quickly made an impact at XYZ Company upon my return to work."

The explanation, should be brief, matter of fact, and behind you. If you over explain and ramble on, then it's obviously still unresolved and needs closure.

If you don't bring it up and they don't ask, be concerned. It could mean that they've already made the decision not to hire you and they're going through the motions.

How do you manage stress or difficult situations?

This is a hypothetical question. It can also be asked like this: Tell us about a time when you were stressed out at work; what caused the stress, what you did to manage it, and the result.

Some jobs are more stressful than others by nature, but they're all stressful at some point or another. Companies want to know how you respond when the going gets tough. They understand it's not a matter of "if" there will be stress, but "when" and "how often."

We all respond to stress in our own way. If you say you don't get stressed, they will have a hard time believing you. This is a "know yourself" or "in touch" question. They want to see how aware you are of your emotions and how you respond when these emotions fluctuate. This is called emotional intelligence, and it is becoming a major factor in hiring decisions. Be prepared to talk about times in your employment/school/life history when circumstances were extremely intense, and how you managed to work through these and still get the job done.

Here is a word of caution. I have seen applicants, who weren't prepared for this question, relive the events while they were answering, and breakdown emotionally during the interview. What the applicant thought they had resolved was in reality still tender and unresolved. Interviews that were going well crashed and burned at this juncture.

Be prepared for follow-up questions to your response. This is a place in the interview where "dive down" questions will be asked to gain a greater understanding of who you are and your level of grit and determination. Companies are fully aware that stress is part of the job, and they want to make sure that you won't be pushed beyond your breaking point.

What are your personal interests or interests outside of work?

This question can really enhance your candidacy. It gives you a chance to talk about some of the personal initiatives you are involved in and how they tie in and compliment the position for which you are interviewing. Involvement in sports and recreation can show you actively take care of yourself and like to compete. Business is competitive, and companies often look for individuals who enjoy competing and who are willing to bring that same spirit to their team.

Being involved in charities and giving back to your community make you an extremely attractive candidate. People who give their time, talent and treasure to those in need are often some of the most successful people in the world. If you think of some people you view as highly successful, you will find in most cases they are passionately involved in volunteer work. They serve on boards of non-profits and give their resources to those causes. When volunteer work is seen on your resume and application, it sends a message that you are passionate about causes beyond yourself and have a focus on making the world a better place. Wouldn't you hire a person who cares about someone or something besides themselves? If you are not currently involved in giving, the good news is it's easy to get started. No matter where you live, the need is great for people to give back to those less fortunate. If you are involved already, don't be shy about letting the company see your passion for your projects. It may even lead to them getting involved in the effort. Many companies now match dollar for dollar and hour for hour that their employees give to charity.

Tell me about a time when:

       -you took the initiative to get something done.
       -you changed someone's mind.
       -you worked as a team to get something done.
       -you had to re-prioritize.
       -you felt you were treated unfairly. (Gotcha!)

In each of the scenarios above, you will need stories you can tell which cover a specific situation or circumstance in which you were involved. You will briefly and succinctly explain the situation, the actions you took, and the results of your actions. One of the frustrating things about these types of questions is that one of your answers could actually satisfy three of the questions asked. Unfortunately you will be expected to respond to all three questions with three different scenarios. The good news is: you already started gathering and developing your stories in Chapter 1!

Do you have any questions for us?

YES! The questions you ask in the interview are as important as the answers you give. Refer to Chapter 3, *Who's Interviewing Who?* for a list of potential questions to ask.

Why should we hire you?

Alas, the Granddaddy of all questions. Let's assume for a moment that up to this point you have been knocking every question they throw you out of the park. You have been precise, succinct, articulate and compelling. If you blow this question, then nothing else may matter. Don't forget that you aren't the only one being interviewed. The competition is fierce. Assume that 10 other people with similar education and experience have already been interviewed, and they were precise, succinct, articulate and compelling as well. It all comes down to: "Why should we hire you?" The next few words you speak are going to determine whether or not you are negotiating salary or sending out more resumes. At this point, most people begin re-listing the attributes they've just spent the last 30 to 60 minutes talking about, like: I'm an ethical, hard-working, team-oriented, do-what-it-takes, individual with an entrepreneurial spirit....blah...blah...blah. They've already heard it. They asked you, "Why should we hire you?" They didn't ask you to summarize everything all over again. Most people remember you by what you say or do last. This is your chance to culminate everything that is great about you into one final closing statement. It would be similar to the closing arguments in a court case. All the facts have been presented. The evidence has been thoroughly examined. Now the attorney stands and delivers his final remarks to the judge and jury whose verdict will determine the fate of their client. This is your closing argument, and the content and strength of your delivery will determine whether or not they hire you or someone else.

Personally, I live for this moment. I consider myself a closer. Not everyone is. I have used a variety of closing statements in interviews, the most memorable being the Michael Jordan story in Chapter 1. As I have progressed in my career and interviewed for higher level positions, the expectation for this moment has increased. The Michael Jordan story was effective coming from a 21 year old recent college graduate, but it might seem a little elementary coming from a seasoned professional. I have developed what has proven to be one the strongest closes that I have ever heard. If it works for me, it may work for you, at least in some variation. You may need to adjust it a little to fit your situation.

"Brooks, why should we hire you?"

I first respond by telling them all of the things that I can do for their organization if they hire me. I don't just regurgitate the listed strengths on my resume. I explain how I can use my strengths and experience to help them achieve their goals. Hiring me is an investment that will yield a return. Companies want to know what it is that you can do for them. Once this argument has been made, I close with the following response which really speaks to my intangibles. This answer opens and closes any window of doubt that I am the right person for the job. I know it works because I have been offered the position 100% of the time since incorporating it into my interviews.

"I am sure since you have been a manager that you have interviewed hundreds of people." *(This lets them know that you understand that they are a competent professional and your fate rests in their hands.)* **"And at some point in your career you may have hired people who looked good on paper and interviewed well, but their lives were revealed to be train wrecks. Their personal problems spilled over into the workplace. You spent 80% of your time running after them and filling their shifts when they were absent, making you less productive."** *(At this point they are visualizing one or more employees in their career whom they have either worked with or hired who was a total mistake. It doesn't matter how careful and meticulous companies are in their hiring practices, at some point they have hired a train wreck. The last thing hiring managers want is to hire another problem child.)* **"And I know that the last thing you want to happen with this hire is to make a mistake. Well my life is pretty normal. I am**

happily married and plan to stay that way. I have two great kids. My wife does an excellent job of building my ego, so I don't need to come to work to have that done. It's taken care of already. I am not bringing any baggage into this position, so when I come to work, I am going to be 100% focused on the job you hired me to do. You get everything you're looking for in a candidate without the baggage." *(Now what I have done is opened up to the interviewers personal information about myself that they are not at liberty to ask. Because of certain laws and regulations, potential employers cannot ask personal questions like: How many kids do you have? How many times have you been married? Tell me about your family? Questions like this can be seen as biased, so companies steer clear of asking these questions, but they would love to know the answers to them. Because the more personal information they know, the more insight they gain into who they are really hiring. Since companies won't ask personal questions, other candidates don't get a chance to really talk about who they are unless they bring it up themselves. By using your personal situation as an asset and a selling point, you are proactively talking about the intangibles that set you apart, and simultaneously relieving the anxiety they have about hiring the wrong person.)*

This honest, forthright approach has proven to be refreshing to those I have interviewed with and provided the extra thrust to push my candidacy over the finish line. Develop your own personal closing argument that discusses the intangibles you bring to the table. If by chance you do have some "baggage" or made some life and career mistakes that were uncovered in the interview, you may consider discussing how much you have learned and grown from those mistakes, and that those experiences have helped develop you into the person and professional you are today. If you are struggling with a particular question or how to address and overcome a unique situation, please feel free to submit it to me at my website. I will do my absolute best to respond as soon as possible.

...interviewing is an open book test...

Wouldn't it be nice to know which questions interviewers were going to ask prior to the interview? Would that be cheating? No. It's called being prepared. So if you want to know the questions interviewers are going to ask, then pay attention to what they have already told you. Remember, the questions are based on the skill sets that companies are looking for in candidates. How do you know which skill sets they are looking for? Go back and take a close look at the job description. Most companies will list for you the requirements they are looking for in a candidate. Make sure you have a story for each required skill set listed on the job description that depicts mastery in those areas, from leadership and organization to communication and persuasiveness. Take the time to write out each story, being sure to describe the situation or task you were involved in, what you specifically did in that situation, and the specific results achieved.

Once you have written these stories down on paper, then you want to practice telling each one aloud. You should be able to tell the story just like you would tell it to a friend at a get together. I encourage people to keep a journal and chronicle some of the major events and projects in which they were instrumental during their high school, college, and professional careers. We can get so caught up in performing at our best that we don't take time to reflect on our accomplishments. Don't sell yourself short. Starting today, begin to chronicle your accomplishments and achievements. Be sure to add any awards and certificates to your brag book, keeping it up to date just like you do with your resume. This makes it so much easier to recall the stories when you need them. When telling your story, be sure to deliver it in a manner that is genuine and not canned. If you answer too quickly after each question, it will seem robotic and rehearsed.

Another tremendous resource to take advantage of is available for free at www.glassdoor.com. In addition to job listings and salary information, they provide interview questions and responses by company and position from actual people who interviewed for those jobs. The site is constantly being updated in real time. Before you go for an interview, it would be a good idea to go to the site and see if there is any information available on the company you are interviewing with. Even if the position you are interviewing for is not listed, you can still gain insight into the interviewing philosophy of the company by looking at how they questioned candidates in other positions.

As we grow and develop professionally, we become wiser and more experienced in how we respond to situations that occur in the workplace. From the first edition of this book to the second, my philosophies on interviewing and how I would answer questions have changed, because I have changed. I plan to continue to grow and progress professionally. Because this process is ongoing, I often make adjustments to how I answer questions before the next edition becomes available in print. You can find updated answer to questions at the blog page of my website at www.brooksharper.com. Be sure to visit often and subscribe, so you can stay updated and continue to improve your interview skills.

POTENTIAL CURVE BALL

I once had a very candid conversation with a hiring manager from one of the largest pharmaceutical companies in the country. He got enjoyment out of interviewing top graduates from elite colleges by questioning them about their GPA's. He would acknowledge their 3.7 or 3.8 GPA and with a very serious look ask them, "What was the problem?" He stated that most candidates break down and fold, not knowing how to respond to criticism of their seemingly strong college performance. Most graduates have no idea that they are simply being asked a gotcha question to see how they respond to it. According to the hiring manager, 95% of them cannot recover from that question which tells him they are likely to fold under pressure in the position.

Action Items and Reminders from Chapter 4

1) Interviewing is an open book test.

2) Do your homework on the organization.

3) Write down your stories and answers to potential interview questions.

4) Practice saying them out loud.

5) Be genuine in your delivery.

Chapter 5
Every Day Is an Interview

Over my career, I have been on countless interviews, whether I was genuinely seeking employment or simply testing the market to see what other opportunities were out there. Though I have a stable work history, I have always been intrigued by other opportunities in the market place and have begun to view interviewing as an extreme sport. I love having options, keeping my options open, and from time to time exercising those options. The best way to have options is to go out and find them, even if you are happy in your current position. Marketing yourself not only keeps you fresh, but aware of the value your experience, skills and abilities have in the workplace. I have been subject to underemployment, underpay, acquisition and downsizing, so I stay sharp and on my toes, not knowing what may lie around the corner. I know people who have been blindsided by a layoff after working for the same company for 20 plus years. Because they haven't hunted a job or interviewed for so long, they have become overwhelmed with the process, given up and stayed unemployed for longer periods of time than necessary. Stay fresh and relevant by testing the market from time to time.

So, YES, I have interviewed with companies sometimes without having any intention of ever going to work for them. Some would argue that this is unethical. I have friends who have given me a hard time about interviewing as a sport, but I take exception to that. First of all, most people find nothing fun about interviewing, though I have acquired a taste for it. Secondly, if I am putting myself through the rigorous interview process, I am investing my time and energy which is extremely valuable to me. As I articulate responses to the interviewers' questions in a fashion that convinces them that I am the best candidate for the position, they have an equal opportunity to convince me why I should leave what I am doing and work for them. Some interviewers approach candidates with a seemingly pompous attitude that we are lucky just to be sitting in their presence. They lose sight of the fact that there are many companies out there looking to hire the best and the brightest, and they need to convince us why their company is the employer of choice. As a hiring manager, even if I know at some point in the interview that a candidate is not going to work out, I would still continue to sell my company as the best employer.

Once, after a strenuous process of interviewing with a Fortune 500 company, I was "fortunate" enough to make it through to the final interview with the Regional Vice President and assistant RVP. From an initial resume sent over the internet, I had been screened by someone in human resources and scheduled to meet with the hiring manager. After our initial meeting, the hiring manager asked me to meet with him again later in the week and bring a sales presentation. I prepared a presentation on his company complete with printed power point slides. *(Whenever asked to give a presentation as part of the interview process, unless otherwise instructed, my presentation is always on the company with whom I am interviewing.)* When

I launched into my presentation, the manager never looked at my presentation slides. He stared into my eyes to see if I was going to look down at my slides as a reference for the information I was conveying to him. To his delight, I knew the material backward and forward. I told him things about his company that showed I had done my homework and was well prepared. Before I turned to the last slide, I said, "Here at _____ we are always looking to bring in the best and brightest talent to our organization. I would like to introduce you to our latest acquisition." I then turned the page to reveal a full page picture of me in a tuxedo. I then used this opportunity to launch into my two minute commercial about myself. His entire demeanor changed as if to say, "This candidate search is over." He wouldn't commit at this point, insisting that there were eight internal candidates he was still considering who were willing to relocate to our market for the position. Nevertheless, he scheduled a field ride for me the following day with his top producing representative. After a day in the field observing, I met with another district manager for what seemed to be a formality. After this I met with the hiring manager again for dinner at one of the nicest restaurants in Columbia, SC. At dinner I asked him how things were going with his other candidates. He looked at me across the table and said, "Brooks, there are no other candidates. You are my candidate!" He shared that of all the folks he had interviewed, I was the person he wanted on his team. I had beaten out 2000 resumes, 40 candidates screened, 10 interviewed face to face, and 8 internal candidates to find myself sitting at dinner, the winner. He proceeded to congratulate me and let me know how fortunate I was, adding that people have a better chance of getting into Harvard Business School than working for his company. Over the course of the meal he told me about the final phase in the interview process and coached me how to be successful. He informed me I would have to drive to Atlanta, GA the next morning and meet with the Regional Vice President and assistant. He cautioned me that it would be tough. He told me to remember everyone's name with whom I came in contact, including the security guards. I was to write the RVP and assistant a thank you card after the interview and leave it with the receptionist.

I drove to Atlanta the next morning arriving at the regional office with plenty of time to spare. I had my thoughts together ready to knock the interview out of the park and anxiously await their offer. The RVP and assistant greeted me with smiles. The smiles were the warmest part of the interview. When I sat down in the interview chair, they began to attack my resume like piranhas. They spent thirty minutes punching holes in my resume, and a very hostile tone was set. It seemed to me that the interview became less about my candidacy and more about them impressing each other. *(I have been successful interviewing and in business for one major reason: I don't think I am better than anyone else, and I don't think anyone else is better than me. I approach everyone with respect and expect the same in return. We're all people.)*

After listening to them for half an hour beat up everything it took me fifteen years to accomplish, I decided to push back, knowing it would probably cost me the offer and disappoint the hiring manger. I felt compelled to defend myself and every other past and future candidate coming before the firing squad. I finally asked them, "Why am I here?" This question took them beyond their comfort zone, and they became defensive. They told me if they hired me, they would be investing $400,000 in me the first year, and they wanted to know how they could be sure I wouldn't leave them in two years. I countered with this statement, "I am prepared to leave a position in which I am highly successful and spend 10 weeks in New York away from my family training with your company; how do I know that you aren't going to lay ME off in six months?" The RVP said, "Well, we can't guarantee that we won't lay you off in six months." I said, "Then I can't guarantee I won't leave you in two years." They were shocked and noticeably flustered. I was surprised that they didn't end the interview right then, but they continued. They said, "How did you find out about this position?" I said, "You posted the opening on the internet." They both began to turn red. The RVP said, "Well, why did you apply for this particular position?" I said, "I want to ask you a question. Your company posts openings for jobs on the internet all of the time regardless if it is truly looking for a candidate or not. Your company does this in order to keep a fresh supply of applicants in the event that you need to fill an opening. In essence, your company is sort of window shopping for talent. Is this correct?" She said, "Well, yes," with an attitude that this was standard business practice and nothing unusual. I said, "Well, that's all I was doing. I was browsing the internet looking at open positions, came across the one you posted and applied. I was window shopping!" The RVP was furious but did keep composure, held it together and the interview ended shortly thereafter. I got thirty minutes down the road, and my cell phone rang. It was the hiring manager. He said, "What happened?" They had undoubtedly briefed him on the interview. I told him that things didn't exactly go as we planned. That was an understatement. In their eyes I had missed out on the opportunity of a lifetime. From my perspective, they had missed out on the candidate of a lifetime. It's important to believe in and respect the management team that you work for, not just the hiring manager. Remember, every day you go to work and labor you are also laboring for the entire company's success. Life is too short to work for mean people. There are plenty of organizations that value hard work, integrity, and robust dialogue, not just someone who is willing to say whatever they want to hear just to get the job.

At this juncture you may have this question: "Isn't this book about saying what is necessary to get the job?" This book is about helping you do and say what is necessary to get the position you were meant for, working with people who respect your effort. During the three hour drive to Atlanta, I was seriously considering going to work for this company, having been very impressed with the company and the team. Yes, the hiring manager sold me. Team Atlanta and I blew the sale.

I have played that interview over and over again in my head. Though I gave as good as I got, I broke one of my own rules and failed to sell them on me and close the deal. It would have been better to humble myself, play their game and win the position. Then I could have declined the offer based on principle. Learn a lesson from my mistake. Always interview to win with the goal of having the final decision in *your* hands.

...every day is an interview...

I have a friend that I used to work with who gets a good amount of entertainment value out of my interviewing exploits. He calls me about once a week and asks, "Where are you interviewing today, Brooks?" My response is always the same, "Every day is an interview."

One time a manager I worked for asked his entire team if any of us were interviewing with other companies. He went around the room and asked us each individually. I was actually shocked and somewhat impressed that he was bold enough to even ask this in a meeting. What really humored me is the fact that he expected someone in that setting to give an honest answer. Seriously, if someone is in the final stages of an interview process, they're not going to say anything for fear of losing the job they currently have. Everyone knows it is easier to find a job while you have a job. Fortunately for me, he went around the room left to right, and I was the last person to be asked. This gave me some time to come up with a strategic response. Surprisingly, I was not in the process of interviewing with any particular company at that time. It would have been interesting to see his face if I would have rattled off about three or four companies with whom I was negotiating compensation packages. Instead, this was my response: "Every day is an interview. I feel that every day I come to work here, I have to work hard and prove to you why you should continue to employ me...." That statement earned a smile from my manger, but it was the second statement that he was not prepared for: "....but at the same time every day that I come to work you have an opportunity to convince me why I should continue to work here." Remember, the door swings both ways!

Every day is an interview! It doesn't matter if you are looking for a new job or not. From the time you go to work for a company, every day you are there is an interview. You are always interviewing for your next promotion or salary increase. You cannot get complacent, because management is constantly evaluating your performance and deciding if you are the person who can move to the next level. I have worked with far too many people who often complained about being overlooked, so they never gave their best effort. Since they never gave their best effort, they *were* always overlooked for promotion. Don't let a negative thought process become a self-defeating prophecy. Always give 100%, and if your efforts go unrewarded, then there will always be opportunities elsewhere for someone with your skill sets.

...EVERY day is an interview...

Once after leaving a speaking engagement, between the venue and my house, my car dropped five quarts of oil. The little red oil light began to flash. I now realize it was a useless warning because as soon as it started flashing, the engine began to lock up. I managed to coast into a car dealership. As one might imagine, I was frustrated, especially given the fact that I had recently spent a considerable amount of money on repairs. I sat in my car debating whether I should put another penny into repairing the car, or scrap it and get another. (*Few things pain me more than dealing with car dealerships and purchasing a car. I'd much rather be interviewing.*) That's when I had an inspirational thought. I got out of my car, walked into the Service Department and managed to find the Service Director sitting in his office. He saw me standing there and said, "Can I help you?" I said, "Do you have your deal making shoes on?" He looked like a kid in a candy store. He got excited and said, "Always!" I said, "My car is broken down in your parking lot, I don't want to pay to have it fixed, but here is what I am willing to do for you: If you fix my car for me, I will help you negotiate your rental uniform contract." (*I have years of experience in contract negotiation in the rental uniform business. Most car dealerships have an agreement with a uniform company which provides uniforms for service technicians as well as a variety of other products and services.*) I assured him that if he allowed me to look at his contract with his current uniform supplier, that I could save him a considerable amount of money--far more than the amount necessary to fix my car. He seemed intrigued by the offer but admitted he was not the person who could make this sort of deal. He told me that only the General Manager of the dealership could agree to such a proposal. He called the GM's office and asked him to come to the Service Department. The General Manager was a sharply dressed guy. He came in, shook my hand and said, "Watcha got?" I explained my proposal, and he said that he didn't hire consultants for his business. He explained that he had contracted with people in the past who didn't give him the expected return on investment. I explained that he would be getting my services at a discount and it would not cost him any out of pocket expense, simply parts and labor to fix my car. After consideration and some pulling and pushing, he agreed to give me $625 toward the cost of repairing my car in exchange for my help negotiating their uniform agreement.

Then he threw me a curve ball. He said, "Have you ever thought about selling cars? We need a guy like you." I countered with, "Will my answer to your question have any bearing on the deal we are making today?" He assured me it would not, and I kindly replied, "No, I am not interested in selling cars." He said, "Not the cars on the lot. I need a guy like you who can build relationships with utility and phone companies. I want to be the number one fleet dealer in the state, and I want you to head up the department." He continued, "I will put an offer together for you and throw in a car, so you don't have to worry about that piece of junk you have sitting in my parking lot!"

I couldn't help but laugh. Here I was trying to get my car fixed without paying out of pocket, and the General Manager was treating this negotiation like an audition for fleet manager.

The point? The job he offered me was not posted on their company website or on a job board site. He was waiting for the right person to come along. I treat every day like an interview, because you never know when opportunity is going to present itself based on the way you handle yourself in a given situation. It may be on an elevator, at a restaurant or the fender bender that you thought would ruin your day. The encounter or chance happening may open a set of doors, that would have otherwise remained locked forever, based on the way you carry yourself and interact with other people every day! Treat every day of your life and career as if you are interviewing for your next promotion, position or salary increase, and you'll always have career options available.

...your name is your brand...

Your name is your most valuable asset! Everything you have done to this point in your life, personally and professionally, good or bad, has had a direct impact on your brand name. When another person hears your name, what adjectives come to their mind? The words others would use to describe you is an indicator of the image your brand projects. If you subscribe to the concept, "Every Day Is an Interview", then you understand that every day, everything you say and do, impacts your brand. This makes you the Brand Manager of your name and image, and it's the greatest responsibility you have in career development. If it's very apparent that you struggle on Mondays and can't wait to leave work on Fridays, then that has a direct impact on your brand. It is essential to place the highest value on your brand name and work relentlessly to enhance it and protect it from anything that could diminish it. Sometimes the brand image we think we project, and the brand image others perceive, are very different. It's incumbent upon you as the Owner and Brand Manager to be aware of that perception, because in many ways it is reality.

Here are some things you control, project and portray that have a major impact on your brand name and image EVERY DAY: Attitude, Work Ethic, Punctuality, Wardrobe, Vocabulary, Body Language, Tone of Voice, How you Respond, Professionalism, Email Address, Voice Mail, Ringtone and Social Media Engagement.

Your ownership of these areas EVERY DAY is the INTERVIEW! Make a commitment to yourself to own and manage your brand. The effective Brand Manager never clocks out or takes vacation from the BRAND! He or she is on the job 24 hours a day, 7 days a week, 52 weeks per year. When promotions and new opportunities present themselves, effective Brand Managers don't have to worry with making wholesale changes to the list above, because it's something they work on EVERY DAY! This is what truly sets you apart from others and gives you a competitive advantage over other candidates.

POTENTIAL CURVE BALL

As a hiring manager, I have done some quirky things to figure out who candidates really were. After the person I was interviewing got to my office, I would ask them to take a seat and tell them I would be right back. I would then slide out of my office into the parking lot, find their car in visitor parking and look. Why? Sometimes where people park, and how, can tell a lot about a person. Also the inside of a person's car can reveal a lot of information about who they really are, and I'm not talking about cleanliness. I once looked into the back window of someone's SUV who was interviewing with another manager I worked with for an outside sales position. In the back of the vehicle were three golf bags. I told the manager, if she hired him, she would never be able to keep him off the golf course. She hired him anyway. She couldn't keep him off the golf course. Be aware of the peripheral things that employers may be observing which can affect the outcome of an interview.

Action Items and Reminders from Chapter 5

1) Treat every day like it is an interview.

2) Every day is an opportunity for you to prove yourself to your employer.

3) Every day is an opportunity for your company to prove itself to you.

4) Make a list of people to let know you are looking for career opportunities and reach out to them.

Chapter 6
12 Keys to Hearing, "You're Hired!"

You are closer now than ever to unlocking the door to your dream job. Use the following keys to open the doors of opportunity, and leverage your talent and experience to gain the position and pay you deserve.

1) The Do's and Don'ts of Resumes

Regardless of where you are in your career - fresh out of high school, college, or a 25-year seasoned professional - you should have an up-to-date resume. Your resume is a living document that never reaches completion. After each promotion, accolade or award, one of the first things you should do is update your resume. Your resume is also an advertisement that markets your knowledge, experience, accomplishments and proficiencies to potential employers. It is not your autobiography, nor should it be written like one. Many people make the mistake of putting far too much information in their resumes. Remember, the average resume that is actually seen by the human eye gets about a 15-second glance. If it is a 1000 word document written in paragraph form, it is almost assured a final resting place in the "NO" file.

Consider the help wanted ads you have seen companies place on their website or on talent search sites. They don't look like an essay or newspaper article, because companies know you're not going to read them. Their job postings are exactly what they look like: professional, strategic marketing pieces designed to capture your attention, and build interest in their company's open positions to attract the best candidates. These ads briefly brand the company, position requirements, and qualifications necessary for employment consideration. Your resume should not be any different. It should quickly brand you, your experience, and what qualifies you to fill their position. Much like the ad you answered caught your eye, your resume should capture the attention of the recipients, giving them a reason to take a longer glance. If your resume is filled with lengthy paragraphs, it may never be read. Think about it; your resume is just one of the 500 that came in that day. The person sorting through them doesn't have the time or patience to read every detail. Your resume should leave people wanting more, not less.

Believe it or not, a company that I am affiliated with recently received a 37-page resume. Are you kidding me? Why not just go ahead and publish it? A commercial for a movie doesn't show a 10-minute trailer; you just see in a minute or two some of the highlights that leave you wanting more. I am a big fan of a one-page resume. When you click on a song on the iTunes store, you don't get to listen to the whole song. On the contrary, you hear a short clip with an option to purchase. Your resume should offer enough information to spark interest and compel the viewer to contact you for an interview, so you can fill in the blanks for them. Keep it simple, and save your "story" for the interview.

When I look at resumes, they often list previous and current positions, followed by the entire job description, copied and pasted from the employer's website. That doesn't spark interest. Your resume should not highlight the activities you have been doing, but the results you have achieved. Anytime you can quantify your results it is helpful. It should list your education, previous employers (including positions held), dates you were there and any accomplishments or awards you received. If you were ranked in the top 10% of sales in your company, then that should be highlighted on your resume. I would caution you about putting quantitative data on your resume, unless you have documented proof of the results. The best companies will expect you to bring proof of your accomplishments to the interview. This is where your credibility binder comes in that we discussed in Chapter 4.

In addition to your resume being captivating, it should also be targeted. Most people have one or two standard resumes they send to every job posting they answer. Remember, you are trying to land your dream job. You can't send the same old resume out to every position. The open position is marketed to a certain pool of talent. If you want to compete with the hundreds of resumes flooding in, you have to customize your resume for the specific job. If you don't personalize it, then it is highly probable your resume will send the wrong message. Send the wrong message? What does that mean? When a general resume comes across the computer screen, it could appear to the screener that you are just fishing or window shopping—You know, sitting at your computer at work, killing time by browsing career websites just to see what's out there. "Oh this looks like a decent gig. Let me loft my basic, generic resume over and see if I get a bite." Professional screeners can see right through this. If you have ever wondered why you didn't get a response after submitting your resume for a job for which you were more than qualified, it may be that your resume was perceived as generic and random. You may have been a solid candidate, but perhaps you didn't take a few minutes to make adjustments to your resume, customizing it for that particular position. If the job is the one you truly want, then take the time to customize your resume to fit the position.

2) Choose References Wisely

Most companies will require three professional and three personal references as part of the interview process. Typically, these references will only be called if the company is serious about making you their final choice. Though very few people would list someone as a reference who would say negative things about them, you still should be cautious in choosing your references. I prefer to use a person as a reference who has sales skills or sales experience. They are usually well-spoken, persuasive, and could easily speak of your attributes, thus enhancing your chances of getting the position. I am often asked to be a reference for people because they know that I am persuasive.

You may also choose references based on the type of position you are applying for. If you know someone who has specific experience in your chosen field, then definitely use this person as a reference. It will lend credibility to your candidacy. This may go without saying, but be sure to let your references know they may be receiving a call from your potential new employer. Not only does this give your references an opportunity to prepare for the call, but it gives you an opportunity to brief them on the type of position for which you are applying and any pertinent information they may need to know beforehand.

INNOVATIVE IDEA!

I have a client who came up with a slam dunk idea for using his professional references to seal the deal and blow the competition away! He was interviewing for a position with a medical device company and wanted to convey how valuable he had been to his previous employer and the doctors whom he served as a representative. He visited his most influential doctors and videoed them singing his praises about the impact his work had on their practices. He also videoed his former manager, and received a glowing reference for being a results-oriented, model employee. He then edited the video, and posted it to YouTube and sent the link to the hiring team he was interviewing with. They were overwhelmed, not only by the references given by colleagues, but the uniqueness and innovation of the idea to create a reference video. They had never seen anything like it! The video pushed him over the top!

3) They're Avoiding "Train Wrecks"

Many interview questions these days are geared to determine why a company shouldn't hire you, as opposed to why they should. In this litigious, lawsuit happy climate, human resources departments are coming up with creative ways to figure out which candidates to avoid.

The last thing any organization wants to bring into its workplace is a train wreck. Train wrecks are people who look good on paper, interview well, but once they are hired it's discovered their lives are "train wrecks". Their personal baggage and problems spill over into the work place, not only making them less productive, but oftentimes paralyzing the entire workplace. Train wrecks slow down their fellow employees by performing inconsistently, showing up late, or not at all. They have a propensity to discuss their personal problems instead of the tasks at hand. Once train wrecks have been hired, it takes months, sometimes years, to weed them out of an organization. Over the course of time, the train wreck's manager becomes frustrated and often has to change working conditions and interoffice rules in order to keep one individual in line. This has a negative effect on the morale of other employees and may run some of the best people off, including the manager.

Human Resources and hiring managers will do whatever it takes to avoid bringing in a train wreck. Due to the way laws are written, employers typically avoid asking certain personal questions. They will ask open-ended questions to see where a candidate may take the answer. Unless you are extremely comfortable with conveying your personal business positively, as demonstrated in Chapter 4, it is best not to bring it up at all.

4) The Power of Saying Nothing

Do not confuse the title of this tip with an attempt to encourage you to stare quietly at the interviewers until your Jedi mind-tricks convince them to hire you. Your use of nonverbal communication and gestures will be as important as what you communicate verbally. I have been training professional speakers for years and have seen speakers transformed from mediocre to magnificent by making subtle adjustments in their nonverbal gestures. When your physical gestures are congruent with your words, it gives the message you're conveying more impact.

Once you have collected stories about yourself that will answer the interview questions, you need to practice incorporating nonverbal gestures into your answers. Using big arm movements when answering questions gives the perception that you are confident in what you are saying. If you are telling them that you went from an entry-level position to supervisor, to department manager, then you want to use large, distinct arm movements to illustrate your progression. When you keep your arms tucked to your side and only use your hands, you look like a Tyrannosaurus rex answering questions. If you're making three points, then hold up your arm and make those points while counting with your fingers.

You want to be relaxed in the interview, but not to the point where it affects your posture. Make sure you are sitting up straight. It's acceptable to cross your legs from time to time as long as it doesn't affect your posture and look awkward. Don't forget to smile, but be real! Allow your personality and excitement to be displayed in your body language. Your nonverbal communication will either enhance your verbal communication or diminish it.

5) Video Yourself

Though I consider myself to be a polished speaker, I was recently reminded that speaking is a craft one never perfects. While reviewing a video of myself giving a presentation, I noticed myself making strange movements with my hands. I was totally unaware. I have always made good use of nonverbal gestures, but this small thing corrected would have made my presentation even more powerful.

Video yourself answering interview questions for practice and you will be amazed at what you see. If you have ever heard a recording of yourself, you may have asked someone else, "Do I really sound like that?" The answer is yes. As shocked as you were at the sound of your own voice, you may be equally amazed at some of the quirky things you do with your body of which you are totally unaware. Take note of the things you observe in the video, and practice working in the nonverbal gestures mentioned above. Doing this will take your interviewing skills to a whole new level.

When I work one-on-one with clients, we always video me interviewing them for the position they want. It is amazing how hitting the record button increases the intensity and helps simulate an actual interview. As we play back the video, clients are amazed at what they see. Sometimes it's difficult for them to watch as they see themselves do things that are typically out of character. I've seen jovial people go through an interview and seem unhappy as if they were about to cry. Videoing allows you to view how you look under pressure and become comfortable with the interview process.

6) Be Likeable

When the interview is over and all the candidates are considered, one of the biggest deciding factors will be whether or not they like you. If they have two equally qualified candidates, the person who was more likeable has a better chance of getting the job. While managers are asking you questions, they are also asking themselves if they can visualize working with you. People enjoy working with those they like, so be likeable. Using tasteful humor in your interview is a plus. I once sang in a mock sales presentation that was a required portion of the interview process. The hiring manager almost fell out of her chair laughing. Not only did I get the offer, but I went to work for her. It turns out that I prefer working for people whom I like as well, especially those with a sense of humor.

Team synergy and chemistry are vitally important when hiring new people. Companies want to make sure the person they are hiring will be a good fit for the rest of the team. So it is possible the company may require you to meet with team members in a group session to get a feel for how you interact with everyone. How well this exchange goes can be the deciding factor in whether or not you get the job. You want to make sure you are genuinely friendly. One of the best things you can do is smile. This sounds simplistic, but smiles are contagious and they set you and others at ease. I have seen people with great smiles fail to use them as a tool, and their true personalities never came out. It is possible to be so focused on what you are saying that you aren't even behaving like yourself. When you video yourself, pay attention to how much or how little you smile.

7) Be Consistent

If multiple people are interviewing you, it is highly probable that at some point all of them will huddle together and have an information exchange. During this meeting they compare notes on candidates and give their feedback on each one. Make sure you are very consistent in your answers to each person interviewing you. Inconsistent answers mean you are inconsistent in other areas of your life, and you may be viewed as dishonest.

8) Brevity is your Friend

Be very concise in your answers. There is nothing wrong with keeping your answers brief and to the point. Sometimes less is more. If you have a tendency to go on and on with your answers, you may notice the interviewer's eyes begin to glaze over. This is because you are putting them to sleep. In addition to being boring, you may end up saying something that costs you—just because you felt you needed to keep talking. Once your answer is given, pause and wait to see if the answer was sufficient. I often ask my interviewers whether or not my response answered their question.

9) Clean it up! Background and Character Checks

It is common, as part of the final interview process, for companies to complete a thorough background check. This would include verification of education, employment history, and credit check. The thought behind the credit check is to see whether or not you are managing your own affairs well. If you're not, the employer may conclude you are not in a position to manage the affairs of their company.

Hiring managers will also search your name online to see what other information is available out there about you which may be pertinent to their decision. Social networking sites can be hotbeds of personal information about a candidate. If you're not careful, what you post could diminish everything you built up in the interview. Be aware that it's not just what the candidate posts online, but the postings of the candidate's associates can play a role as well.

I was scheduled to speak to a large group of educators on a college campus and researched the school online before my arrival. At the home page of the school's website they were celebrating their student of the month. This included a professional headshot and well-written article about the student. I googled the students name to see if the article at the homepage of the school's site was strong enough to appear in Google. It would have been a great illustration of how this type of article enhances the student's internet presence and boosts the candidacy for positions upon graduation. Sure enough, the third link on Google was the article about the student being honored by the school. Unfortunately, the student's Facebook and Twitter profiles were 1st and 2nd. The tweets of the student were explicit in nature overshadowing the accolades from the article. This type of scenario is occurring far too often! Great potential employees are missing out on tremendous career opportunities because their personal lives, played out on social media, detract from their professional profile. Make sure your personal and professional online presence match.

10)   Find a Coach

I have been fortunate in my career to be surrounded by good mentors who helped coach and train me. Without their guidance, my success would be marginal at best. In most of the interviews that I have been on, I have relied on coaches to help walk me through each phase. The idea I shared about giving a book to the hiring manager in Chapter 4 was bounced off of three different people before I made the decision to do it. Getting as far as I have with some of the most exclusive companies in the United States was a result of tapping into the knowledge and experience of industry experts. The greatest athletes in every sport have all had at least one thing in common: Coaches! I encourage you to find a successful person in your chosen field who is willing to give you advice, even if you have to pay for it. I have a friend in the speaking industry who paid a substantial amount of money to be mentored by an expert in the industry. He didn't view the money he spent as an expense, but rather as an investment. His initial investment in a coach has yielded returns that were initially inconceivable. I am extremely grateful to have been associated with people who were willing to offer their time and talent to help me succeed. Choose the people who mentor and influence you wisely, because their advice can make the difference in your future.

11)   Negotiating Salary and Accepting the Offer

Talking about money, for some reason, seems to make many job seekers nervous. I can appreciate this to some extent, but it is time to get beyond it. At some point it is going to come up, and you have to be prepared to discuss it. The job seeker wants to make as much money as possible, and the company views payroll as an expense that has to be controlled. If you are asked what your salary requirement is, you don't want to sell yourself short and you don't want to state an amount so high it prices you out of the market. So, what is the right formula? When should you discuss money? It is my preference, when interviewing with a company, to discuss money as late in the game as possible. I don't talk about money unless they bring it up. My reasoning for this is simple. I view the interview as my opportunity to sell myself to them and convince them, beyond a shadow of a doubt, that I am the perfect person for the position. If money is discussed too early in the interview process, then I may not have had enough opportunity to do this. Once I have convinced them that I am the right person, then they are tasked with putting a package together (Salary & Benefits) which will convince me to accept their offer. In the event they ask your salary requirements early on in the interview process, then you may want to use one or both of the following responses:

"I expect to be paid fair market value for this position based on my experience and abilities."

and/or

"Though salary is important to me, it's not the only thing that I take into consideration. I will be looking at the total package including: salary, benefits, upward mobility, longevity, etc."

Once an offer is made....Congratulations!!!! You did your job! You won! Now the hard part begins. You have to decide whether or not the money they have offered you is worth your time, energy, and effort. Only you can make this decision. When I consider an offer, I look at several things that are important to my value system. Usually money is the last thing in my consideration. Flexibility and enjoyment are the most important things to me in a position. Will I be able to make my kids' ball games, recitals, plays, etc? Will I enjoy the actual work I will be doing? Can I envision myself working for the person who will manage me? If he or she is a micro-manager, then I know it is not going to work and I would decline the offer.

By the way, even if I know early on in the interview process that I will probably decline an offer, I almost always finish the process and sell myself to the fullest extent for this reason: If and when I walk away from the offer, I want them to know that they let the best candidate get away. The only thing better than getting a six-figure offer is turning one down for the right reasons, because it's a fulfilling feeling to know that you can't be bought.

Some other things I consider in an offer are vacation time, health insurance coverage and cost, retirement and tuition reimbursement. I suggest that you make a list of things that you value in a position and then rank them from most important to least. It is rare that an offer meets all of your expectations, but if it hits the most important ones, then it may be worth accepting. Remember to look beyond salary and calculate the total compensation package.

12) Negotiating Salary for a Promotion

It's an exciting thing to be valued enough by the company you work for to be offered to take the next step up the ladder. If you are being offered a promotion, it is a testament to your hard work and the results you have produced. Just because you are offered more money for a new position, however, doesn't mean it is a good deal for you.

With the first promotion I received in my career, I actually took a base salary decrease of more than 25% of my pay. I was sold on the idea that moving into management was a tremendous opportunity to advance higher in the company ranks. The promotion was proposed as a stepping stone which eventually would lead to higher earnings, far surpassing the entry-level position I had been in. Though there was some merit in that theory, I naively accepted the first offer they gave me, and jumped at the opportunity to lead a team and drive results. I was under the false belief that the amount of money I was offered was the best the company could do for me. I assumed the manager had fought for every dollar he could get his hands on. Shortly after accepting the position, my manager was replaced. The new manager reviewed my salary and told me that I had been underpaid, and that I had left money on the table which could have been in my paycheck. Lesson learned.

Since then, there have been other offers for promotion, but I have never accepted the initial offer. I know now that there is always a little more they can do. In my experience, when companies offer salaries for promotion, it is typical for them to focus on the amount of the increase as opposed to the total dollar amount offered for the position—much like a car salesman may try to sell a customer on the amount of the car payment instead of the total price of the car. Even if you are offered a 20-40% increase to take on new responsibilities, it doesn't necessarily mean the total amount offered is commensurate with the position and duties you are being asked to perform. If you are not comfortable with the offer, it may be better to say so and decline it than to accept and regret it. Six months into your new position, when you hit the first set of road blocks and adversity, if you were not happy with the offer you accepted, then you may experience buyer's remorse.

Whatever dollar amount you are making currently, or in your previous positions, the amount you make or made is what you accepted. In life, we get what we accept, so don't accept something that you are going to regret. It is far better to walk away from an offer, than to accept it and let it eat at you for the duration of your employment. The organization will respect you more for not accepting an offer than settling for less than you deserve. Don't allow temporary financial circumstances to cloud your vision and reasoning when considering your offer. You have to live with the amount you accept, so make sure its something you are comfortable with and won't regret. That said, you also should consider the long-term value of a promotion. Though you may not receive the offer you expected, the new position could lead to higher earning potential in the long run. The experience of the position can prove to be invaluable, and showing progression in your career enhances your resume and makes you more attractive and marketable to other companies.

Action Items and Reminders from Chapter 6

1) Video yourself doing a mock interview.

2) Make a list of everything you are expecting in a position (benefits, growth opportunities, stability, flexibility, responsibility, etc.) and rank them from most important to least important.

3) Start or continue to develop your public speaking skills. You never know when one of the requirements of the interview process will be to give an oral presentation to a group.

4) Clean and sweep any social website messes.

5) Find a career coach.

6) Determine your expected salary and the least amount you are willing to accept.

Chapter 7
Why Didn't They Hire Me? (A Dozen Reasons!)

If you are like many, you may be scratching your head wondering why you weren't hired after having such a great interview. You were so close, and now it's back to the drawing board. I have good news: It's not a total loss if you do a fair assessment and learn to be better prepared for the next interview.

Here are a DOZEN reasons interviews don't yield the result expected:

1. Not clearly communicating your value

Companies don't pay people for time, but for the value they bring. Invest time and energy thinking about what makes you different from everyone else and why you would be a valuable member of the team. Be able to persuasively answer, "Why should we hire you?" If you don't know why or genuinely believe in your value, then you are going to have a hard time convincing the company to choose you.

2. Not being yourself in the interview

From the awkward handshake to the sweaty forehead—You sat down and your personality fled the room! Personality and likability play a huge role in hiring decisions. Relax! Compose! BE YOURSELF! Remember, the worst they can say is no.

It is important that the company interviewing you see the real you, not the nervous version you morph into the moment you sit down to interview. The more you practice and hone your interview skills, the better at interviewing you become. Familiarity with the process allows you to remain calm and stay within your true character, helping portray the real you.

3. Shying away from and minimizing your achievements

An interview is one of those unique times when it is perfectly acceptable and expected to highlight your accomplishments. I work with many clients, who not only struggle with discussing their value, but have trouble **seeing** their value. Every life experience you go through, and everything you have ever accomplished, should be considered when constructing your resume and presenting your value in the interview. Sometimes the thing you think is small and irrelevant, because it's simply "who I am" and "what I do", is actually the rare and unique thing that pushes you over the top and wins the job!

You have to highlight your accomplishments and sell your value! I worked with a client who struggled to see the value and relevance of being awarded ROTC cadet of the year, out of hundreds of participants, while in college. Not only was it not included on his resume, but he refused to bring it up or highlight it in the interview as proof of exceptional performance worthy of commendation. Your achievements are only small and insignificant if you leave them out. Present your value with confidence telling how it can make a difference for the company, but don't be overconfident or arrogant.

4. Overconfidence

No one wants to work with a know-it-all. You can't teach them anything because they believe they're the smartest people in the room. It's no wonder that one of the top qualities Google looks for when hiring employees is humility. It's a characteristic that signals you will be open to other people's ideas and willing to learn, grow and develop. You want to talk about your achievements and value in the interview with humility.

5. Unprepared

Preparation determines interest level. If you go into the interview and "wing it" because you believe it's "in the bag" or just a formality, don't be surprised when you don't get the offer. The truth is you may have sabotaged your chances unknowingly, and never know if you would have gotten the offer had you better prepared

You can leave nothing to chance. There are other candidates who understand they're competing against you. They are going above and beyond in preparation to set themselves apart and differentiate themselves from the others. Mediocre candidates who are well prepared, often get the job over unprepared perfect candidates. Companies appreciate those who come prepared, having done everything possible to ready themselves for the interview. Make sure you've done your homework on the company, and can articulate why you want to work for them and why they should hire you!

It's not a good feeling when you leave the interview knowing you could have done much better—knowing you didn't invest enough into the opportunity. Instead of celebrating your performance, you're disappointed and regret not didn't doing everything possible, and that they didn't see your BEST. Well-prepared candidates have a certain sense of calmness about them that unprepared candidates don't, and it's noticed in what they say and how they say it. BE PREPARED!

6. Failure to address that ONE thing

Did you ask if there were any concerns about your candidacy? Most applicants don't. It is perfectly OKAY to inquire about any hesitancy the company may have about hiring you or if there is anything during the interview that needs more clarification. Once you are out the door, it is too late. Talk about it while you have their attention. If there is an "elephant in the room" and they haven't brought it up, it's not because they haven't noticed it. When you proactively address potential concerns, it's refreshing and appreciated because the guesswork is taken away.

I received an inquiry from a job seeker who had been fired from a previous position due to a customer complaint. Though he has learned from his mistake, he struggles discussing it when it is brought up in an interview. This can be extremely frustrating, because it may seem that this will follow you the rest of your career. (Remember, Every Day is an Interview! The choices we make in our current positions have a profound impact on future opportunities!) But all is not lost!

First of all, it's an expensive lesson to learn, but also a valuable one. The person you become as you work through and overcome a blemish to your resume, not only makes you a stronger candidate, but a wiser employee. Being terminated from a position for insubordination or misconduct can be perhaps the best thing that ever happens to a person. Perhaps the wake-up call from being let go is the catalyst for necessary change that otherwise may have never taken place. There is a book written by several famous authors entitled, *We Got Fired! ...And It Was The Best Thing That Ever Happened to Us.*[1] I encourage you to check it out if you fall into this category.

More than likely, being fired will affect some opportunities, especially immediately following the termination. In time, your performance that following the termination will provide cover for previous mistakes. In the short term you may have to settle for a lower position and work your way back. Spend some time practicing talking about the situation and, more importantly, what you learned from it. In your explanation be sure to take complete responsibility for your actions. In no way should your response sound like a justification or an excuse for your behavior. Own the mistake and move on! If in any way you sound like you're trying to blame someone else for your response, it signals to the interviewer that you still don't "get it." Being proactive is the best approach, because it allows you to control the narrative. When you bring it up, be brief in your explanation; don't ramble.

One of the most successful professionals I have ever worked with was hired by our company upon release from prison, following a felony conviction. He was hired into an entry-level position for which he was more than qualified. It was the only way he could begin to repair the damage he had done to his reputation and resume. His previous indiscretions were quickly overshadowed by his performance. He received promotion after promotion, eventually landing a VP position in a totally separate industry. It takes time, tenacity and perseverance, but overcoming blips in your employment and background can be done. Face it head on in the interview process, be upfront, and willing to do what may seem remedial until you re-establish your credibility.

7. Rambling

WONK, WONK, WONK! Don't go on and on and on and on. When you eat up too much time on one question, it doesn't leave time for the rest of the interview. Keep your answers concise.

8. Poor follow through

Be sure to send a handwritten note thanking everyone for their time and consideration. An email gets tossed into the "Sea of Sameness" with everyone else's. When you take the time to handwrite a note, stick a stamp on it and mail it, it is so much more personal and impactful. Professionals appreciate those who are thoughtful enough to mail a thank you card.

I know what you are thinking! What if they make the hiring decision before the card gets there and it's too late for it to impact the decision? Send the email right away, and your thank you card can follow it and be the icing on the cake. The email will also help alleviate the anxiety of waiting for the card to arrive in the mail.

9. It was over before it started

The company had a pre-determined candidate they planned to hire before you ever walked in. There is nothing you could have said or done to change their mind. The posting of the position and the "search" for qualified candidates was only a formality. They knew exactly who they were going to choose before the process began. This happens all the time. There isn't much you can do about it in the interview, but you can learn a valuable lesson from it.

I have worked with many clients who have been disappointed to learn the job or promotion they were applying, or interviewing, for had a chosen candidate before their name was ever in the hat. My advice to them is to remember this simple truth: Every Day Is an Interview! The person whom the company has already decided to hire or promote had been interviewing long before the position posted. They got the job because they were either performing at a high level in their previous position(s) or networking with the decision makers. They sold themselves in advance of the position becoming available.

The best interview you will ever have is performing at your best every day. So many people only begin to perform well when it's time for their performance review or promotion. They seem to forget or ignore their performance was not exceptional prior to the opportunity.

If you feel you're up against insurmountable odds and the decision has been predetermined, always give your best interview anyway. Make them wish they had hired or promoted you! Though you may not change their mind this time, you may be interviewing for the next position or promotion right around the corner.

10. Not asking for the job

In order to G-E-T you have to A-S-K. The most fundamental thing you will do in the interview is ASK for the job. Part of convincing them to hire you is showing them you want it bad enough to ask. Don't fake yourself out with mind games, thinking if they want you, they'll ask you. You will be setting yourself up for disappointment. Some people never even put their name in the hat for promotions. They expect to be chosen because they feel entitled. Don't be naive! Let them know you want it by applying and asking. This shows you're genuinely interested in actually doing the job.

11. It didn't go as well as you thought

Reality Check – When I work one-on-one with clients, I'm usually the first call they make after their interview. Typically, they'll call and begin to tell me how well it went overall. They affirm that many of the questions we studied and prepared for were the exact questions asked in the interview. However, once we start diving down into the details of their answers, and their execution of the little things that make a big difference, they admit there was room for improvement.

Sometimes is doesn't go as well as you think. Perhaps the answers you give, which in most cases would have been homeruns, simply weren't what they were looking for in this case.

12. It wasn't meant for you

Just because you could have gotten the job and would have been great at it, doesn't mean it was a great fit for you. If they would have offered you the job, you may not have been able to walk away, even if instinctively you knew it wasn't the right fit. You wouldn't have been able to resist. Sometimes the company picks up on this during the interview. Though you were perfect on paper and hit the interview out of the park, they sensed something that signaled you were not the person they should hire.

I have worked with clients in this same situation. One in particular was convinced that his dream job had become available and that my services were required to push him over the top. His resume was impeccable, he interviewed well and pulled all the right internal and external networking levers. As I got to know this person better throughout the process, I discovered if he indeed accepted the offer it would cost him a great deal personally. It would be over an hour commute and an eventual move away from key people in his life who needed him to be in close proximity. That distance would have created an emotional strain that could have very well affected his job performance. He was so convinced this was the opportunity of a lifetime, he was willing to overlook the personal implications and accept any offer. I was relieved for him when they offered it to another candidate. Sometimes the position isn't right for you, and the good news is: There is something even better right around the corner! Chapter 8 is all about turning the corner and your passion into your paycheck!

POTENTIAL CURVEBALL

I was interviewing a candidate once with an impressive resume. He was sharply dressed and well spoken. The one piece of advice I would have given him if I were coaching him would be this: "Take off the Figaro bracelet and stop karate chopping the desk to add emphasis to every word." To really get the picture, I would have to demonstrate it for you. But he kept doing this karate chop on the table and each time he did, the bracelet would clink against it. It became a distraction and subtracted from what he was actually saying. Accessories are nice as long as they don't become the focus and detract from what you are saying and your goal of getting the job.

Action Items and Reminders from Chapter 7

1) Make a list of your skill sets and life experiences, and be able to discuss how each one can bring potential value to the position and how it aligns with the goals of the company hiring you.

2) Review the video of your mock interviews and make sure your personality and true self is on display. If you don't like what you see, do it again until the real you is captured.

3) Make a list of personal and professional achievements, no matter how small you think they may be. Practice discussing them with a partner or on video.

4) PREPARE! Don't "WING IT!"

5) Practice ASKING for the JOB! Know how you are going to phrase your A-S-K.

6) Handwrite your Thank You note.

7) Do a thorough, honest assessment of how well the interview went. Acknowledge the areas where you performed well and the areas that need improvement.

8) Keep improving your interview techniques.

CHAPTER 8
Turn Your Passion Into Your Paycheck

I worked in an industry for 10 years in which I made a comfortable living and gleaned invaluable experience, but I was miserable. Every Sunday evening around 4:00 pm, I would begin to get a sick feeling in my stomach. That feeling was the angst from having to go to a job the next day that I couldn't stand. I worked in a cutthroat environment where you were only as good as the current day's performance. I gave ten years of my career, only to hear, "What have you done for me lately?" It seemed I was always one lost account or wrong decision away from losing my job. It kept me on my toes, but it was no way to live my life. My manager used to tell me, "What doesn't kill you, will make you stronger," but it began to feel like a slow death. When I would go on vacation, it would take about four days for me to finally turn the job off in my mind and start enjoying it. I knew something had to change.

Then someone asked me a simple question I had never thought of. This question was the catalyst that helped me plot a new course in my career: "If you could write your own job description, what would it be?" I couldn't answer that question. I had never really taken the time to consider what I would really enjoy. If I were given a pen and a piece of paper and told to write my own job description, and that's what my job would become, what would it be? This question helped me realize I had been going about my career completely wrong. I was like many people who decide what they want to do by looking at help wanted ads. Instead of writing my own job description, I was settling for the job descriptions other people had written, and I was not alone. Today when people ask me what I do for a living, I tell them I am an "Edutainer." "Edutainment" is the fusion of education and entertainment. Ever since I wrote my job description, I have asked many people to do the same. It rarely occurs to people that they have the freedom and liberty to write their own job description and gain employment by doing it.

I have come to the realization that if I work 40 hours a week for 35 years, I will have spent 72,800 hours at work. (These are conservative numbers for me.) If I'm going to put that much of my life and energy into something, then I might as well enjoy what I am doing. I have always wanted to labor with a sense of purpose. Sure, I am as interested in making a good living as anyone else, but I want to be passionate about what I am doing. I decided to turn my passion for helping others into my paycheck.

For you, it may be that you're just sick and tired of that feeling you get at 4:00 p.m. every Sunday afternoon. The one where reality of another week of working at a company, doing a job that you cannot stand, answering to someone who does not appreciate you, and collecting a wage that barely pays the bills, sets in. You may have arrived at a place where it's not about money, you're just ready to do something you truly enjoy and can be passionate about.

I talk to high school and college graduates who have no clue what they want to do in terms of a career. I talk to middle-aged men and women who have been working approximately 15 years, and many of them still have no idea what they want to do with the rest of their lives. They just know something has to change. Sadly enough, I speak with folks nearing retirement who have more regrets than dreams.

I encourage you to sit down with a pen and a piece of paper and write your own job description. Put in writing what you are passionate about. The result of this process becomes the foundation for your search. The desire to do what you love, not only will set you apart in an interview, but will fuel your success once you get the job. If you are interviewing for something you are 100% given to, then your conviction will be the extra juice that persuades a company to hire you instead of another candidate.

To the recent graduate, I give this advice: Start small; think big. Don't expect to graduate and land a job making $100,000 per year, sitting in a corner office, driving a company car. Have the mentality that you are willing to get your foot in the door in an entry-level position in order to have the opportunity to prove what you can do. Cream always rises to the top. If you are willing to work harder than everyone else doing what it is that you love, then it will not take long for the right people to notice.

Keep your cost of living as low as possible early in your career. This will give you more leverage and the flexibility to walk away from bad situations. Far too many graduates, shortly after finding a job, run out and buy a house, car, furnishings and then can barely afford to eat. It isn't long before they begin to dislike their job, because their entire paycheck is consumed supporting the lifestyle they have created. Be patient in purchasing these items. Don't fall prey to predatory lenders, who are willing to help you purchase all at once the things it took your parents a lifetime to acquire.

To the seasoned professional, who is sick and tired of being sick and tired, turning your passion into your paycheck can be a little more complicated. One of the reasons I worked a job I didn't enjoy for so long is because I had created a lifestyle which required a certain amount of money to maintain. Credit cards, student loans, car payments, and other poor discretionary spending habits created a situation that seemed inescapable. I finally drew the line in the sand. I made a decision to take control of my finances and sacrifice creature comforts to get out of debt, so I could control my future. It wasn't easy, but what a liberating feeling it was the day I paid off my last debt!

I have friends who work jobs they cannot stand, and I challenge them to find something they're passionate about. Sadly I often get this response: "I'm stuck. I can't do something else, because I can't afford to take a pay cut." Their hyper-consumption and consumer debt have forced them to do a job they seemingly hate to maintain their life-style. They feel that they have no other options. Oftentimes their frustration isn't with their employer, but with themselves for making poor financial choices. If they had no debt and an "I Quit" fund (six months of living expenses in savings), they might view their job in a totally different manner. They wouldn't wake up each morning and head to work motivated by the fear of losing everything they have, but would go to work by choice. That in itself can make your job more enjoyable. In all actuality, people, whose paychecks primarily go towards paying their debts, don't really work for their employer. On the contrary, they actually work for the organization from whom they borrowed the money. Their employer is simply a source of revenue to pay their real employer: the bank or credit card companies. It is an undeniable fact that the borrower is servant to the lender. If you are in this situation, then be willing to sacrifice for a period of time in order to take control of your career and future.

Action Items and Reminders from Chapter 8

1) Do a personality assessment.

2) Write your own job description.

3) Tighten up your finances.

Final Thoughts
Passion Is Found in Purpose

One of the most fulfilling things in this world is to know that your life has meaning. The closer people arrive at achieving their potential and purpose, the greater their self-worth and confidence become. In contrast, the further people are away from their potential and purpose, the lower their self-worth and the greater their doubt.

A good practice for everyone is to assess themselves and their situation often. As selfish and vain as some are, it's amazing how little they actually consider, inventory, and assess their situation. Ask yourself the following questions: What am I good at? What do I enjoy? How can I find a career which allows me to enjoy doing what I am good at, while making the money I need to live the lifestyle I want?

There are many assessments you can take that really pinpoint the type of person you are, based on your personality and the way you think. Participating in these types of tests can give you a clearer view and add some color to the career that is right for you. One of the best personality profiles available is the Myers-Briggs Personality Assessment. This assessment can also offer insight on what influences and motivates you. It may be that your personality and willingness to take chances is indicative of an entrepreneur, and you should be focusing your efforts on writing a business plan, as opposed to a career plan. Perhaps you are a team player, and you may not find fulfillment in a managerial role. Personality assessments are simply a few clicks away on your computer. In many cases these assessments are available for free.

Everyone has strengths and areas of opportunity for improvement. It may be helpful to take a piece of paper and draw a line right down the middle. On one side write your strengths, and on the other side write your weaknesses. This list will come in handy when preparing your resume and eventually in interviewing. Regardless of your strengths and weaknesses, there are qualities available to every person that can bring value to any company worth its salt: **integrity, character, and diligence.** Show me a person with these three qualities, and they have the ingredients necessary to be on my team.

Integrity

Integrity is being honest with yourself and others; being able to look people straight in the eye with sincerity. This quality, by far, is the single largest need and deficiency in business today. Unfortunately, we work in a world that far too often compromises integrity for results, or what is right for expediency. More value should be placed on the integrity of your name than any amount of power and money you could acquire. What do people think of when they hear your name? You spend a lifetime building your name, and it can be reduced to nothing with one poor decision. People with integrity are perceived as genuine, a quality that is refreshing and increasingly rare. When a company starts making final decisions on which candidates of similar education and experience they will hire, the candidate who is the most genuine will be in higher demand. Though a person can prepare themselves to ace an interview, it is very difficult to fake being genuine. Many times the people conducting the interview aren't just listening to what you're saying, but simply trying to figure out if what you are telling them is true or not. Organizations want to hire people who are who they say they are. I recall Notre Dame University hiring a very capable football coach, only to fire him a week later because he lied on his resume. It is far better to tell the truth and face the consequences than to lie and damage your name. It would be better to lose everything you own and maintain your integrity than to be the richest person in the world and be a liar.

Character

As important as integrity is, your character carries significant weight as well. Character is who you are when no one else is watching. The things you place value in are determined by your character. Good character gives a person the ability to overcome prejudice and allows for appreciation of people for who they are. Character is a critical component of discretion, discernment, attitude, and appropriateness. Without strong character, a person has a tendency to weaken when adversity presents itself, and their judgment may be impaired when tempted. There will be many circumstances in your job where you will be entrusted by the company you work for to represent them. They will need to have absolute confidence that you will do so without compromising their values and principles.

Diligence

Some people spend more time, effort, energy, and creativity trying to get out of work than if they would have just done what they were supposed to do in the first place. Remember, that every day is an interview, so the hard work you put in today may be the element that earns you the promotion tomorrow.

Regardless of your purpose in life, if you lack integrity, character, and diligence it doesn't matter how successful you think you are; your life will lack true fulfillment.

Turning your passion into your paycheck will take thought and time to accomplish. With the right combination of information, planning, commitment and action, you can do what you love and get paid to do it. By applying the concepts in this book you are better prepared to answer the question, "Why should we hire you?" There is no substitute for immediate action. Start building your future today!

Bibliography

Chapter 4: They've Got Questions, You've Got Answers

    1.   Sam Parker & Mac Anderson *212° The Extra Degree* The Walk the Talk Company April 2006

Chapter 7: Why Didn't They Hire Me? A Dozen Reasons

    1. Harvey MacKay *We Got Fired! – and it's the best thing that ever happened to us* Ballentine Books September 2004

NOTES